HOW
TO MURDER
A
MINISTER

HOW
TO MURDER
A
MINISTER

PASTOR X

Fleming H. Revell Company
Old Tappan, New Jersey

To the Church in my house,
Mary, Marsha and Karla

Preface

The sign on my door reads "Pastor." I was reared in a home that loved to entertain the pastor, and twice a year, at the times of revival meetings, our home was open to the pastor and his visiting evangelist. My brothers and I would stand back in awe when these distinguished gentlemen came into the room.

Little did I realize in those early years that God was going to impress on my heart a call to the pastoral ministry. The decision to become a minister was made during my sophomore year in high school. In my denomination one can be ordained without a theological degree, and so it was with me. Before I reached my nineteenth birthday a church had extended to me an offer to be its pastor. I considered that day a great day in my life.

At the close of the evening service of my second Sunday I was told to leave the room, that a vote would be taken.

Presently, a deacon came outside where I was nervously pacing about, and told me to come in. Upon entering the room, I was told that the church had voted to extend to me the office of pastor. No mention was made of my duties. Preaching twice on Sunday, conducting funerals, visiting the sick and shut-ins, and hearing wedding vows were what *I had heard* were a pastor's duties. Nevertheless, I was given a job and no instructions to go along with it. No hours were established and no schedule was made. I was a pastor, so they said.

There were sixty-five people present that night, and now, after these many years, I am sure there were at least that many ideas as to what my duties were, especially as those duties related to each individual personally.

"Pastor"? I am still trying to find out what that word really means. Though I was told in college and in the two theological seminaries I attended, the role is still vague.

Too often a local pastorate is what *the people want it to be.* The voice of the pastor on Sunday and the duties he performs are molded by the confused mind of the people. As a lad I witnessed the dismissal of three of my pastors. In each case the pastors "had been here long enough" or "didn't fit in very well" or "just weren't good mixers." The truth of the matter was that each man was an individual and could not adjust to the image the people had of a "real" pastor.

As pastors, we do actually live in what has been called a "goldfish bowl" world. The sad thing about most fish in a bowl is that they either go around in a circle or dart aimlessly, never cutting the same path twice. They jump at every finger that touches the bowl, or what is worse, follow the moving fingers around the bowl. One of the strangest things a fish in a bowl will do is back away in seeming fear of a menacing hand. The tremendous sense of insecurity of many pastors is heartrending as they look with fear at the fingers on the bowl.

The church, as statistics point out vividly, is in dire need of young men to dedicate themselves to the ministry. My own denomination ordained only one-half as many last year as it did ten years ago. Our young men are fearful of the pastorate, partly because of the abuse that has been administered by many churches.

The difficulty is that we have not defined the role of a pastor either to the people or to ministerial candidates. The authority, if any, a pastor enjoys is not clearly understood. Even sadder is the fact that many of our young people, not knowing what the pastoral duties are, grow up in a church without respect for the pastor. It reminds me of a statement a high school boy sneeringly made to his pastor concerning the addition of a room to the parsonage. The pastor had offered to help, and the young lad remarked, "You work? My dad says preachers never work." His dad was the son of a minister and a leading steward in the church.

It has been aptly stated that the problems facing modern man will ultimately fall into the spiritual area of investigation, because science is so rapidly forcing men to reinterpret and restate their positions on just about every matter under the sun. If we agree that the perplexities facing men will at last find their roots in theology, then we come to the connecting link between men with their problems and the spiritual area that these problems involve. In other words, if men have needs that are ultimately spiritual, who is the one to minister to these men? Because philosophers and theologians minister to the layman mainly through books, the only person who truly serves as the connecting link between the world of men and the world of ideas is the parish minister.

Contents

HOW
TO MURDER
A
MINISTER

1

The Frustrations of the Pastor

I receive a constant stream of letters from cl rgymen who are so frustrated in their work that they a sire some kind of change in vocation.—D. ELTON TRUEBLOOD

Can it be true that the most confused and frustrated group of people in the country today are the local pastors? This has been stated in one way or another in the many books on the general subject of the renewal of the Christian ministry and the renewal of the church. If this statement is too general, it still must be conceded that there is enough truth in it to merit serious consideration of the problem.

Something is wrong and badly in need of correction. Many persons vehemently deny that any problem can exist with the pastorate and this on very good grounds, or so it seems. They say that the ministry is God-ordained and there can never be a serious shortage of ministers—if there is, it is not the churches but the pastors who are at fault. These people offer easy solutions, one of which was published by a denominational paper in a recent article on the need for establishing a system for filling needed pulpits. A system was suggested for securing candidates for small congregations. This was met with hostility, one letter to the editor proclaiming that the Holy Spirit would provide men who were God-called and that "professional" preachers were not God-called. "Professional" preachers were men who had stated that they would be available for preaching.

So, the frustration of the pastor is seen first in that a great segment of the church will not allow problems to be aired. There is a real and pressing problem in numbers today. There are just too few pastors to go around. The shortage will continue to be acute as the years go by. Many laymen who have served on pulpit committees or their equivalent can sadly attest to this fact, and no pious or handy answer will completely satisfy. Even such statements as a "God-called ministry" do not adequately govern our frustrations. In fact, these can easily add to one's frustrations.

Some of the frustrations are worthy of our attention and the first is most critical. The pastor is in a historical succession to one of the most misunderstood and undefined positions in our modern society. To a great extent the role of the pastor is misunderstood on the part of society both *inside* and *outside* the church. This creates such a pressure on the average man that his abilities are greatly hindered by its very weight. Although the individual pastor is not sure of all his duties, most are sincerely searching for a definition of that lofty office.

Some would ask, "Doesn't the New Testament define his duties?" That the writers of the New Testament documents envisioned the institutional ministry as we know it today is not likely. The concepts of prophet and priest are implied in his office, but these characteristics are seen only fleetingly. Most references to the pastoral office in the New Testament deal with how the pastor is to *act* or *be* rather than what he is to *do. Here is the heart of the problem.* Much is said about the kind of men the church needed but nothing of guidelines for his role or duties; which is understandable because of the infancy of the church and the newness of the pastoral office. The Old Testament is even less helpful in attempting to develop a concept of the Christian pastor.

This lack of job description is overcome to some extent for the minister who teaches in college or in a seminary. What his students think of him is important but does not color his work nearly as much as the congregational response to the pastor. The frustration of the lack of role definition within the New Testament is a real problem because the pastor is called on to start here at the heart of the written revelation of God. Within the very Book from which his work flows there is an understandable lack of job description because of the nature of its parts. What is specified is so general that sometimes laymen make easy and over-simplified conclusions as to what their pastor does. Laymen who are actively engaged in church work and Bible exposure come to the conclusion that "preachers" have it easy, which conclusion places great stress on the pastor.

This is not an isolated idea. It is so prevalent that most any day at least one layman will make a crack at the "do-nothing role" of the pastor. Now, the layman in question knows what a pastor *is to be* because he will pardon himself for an off-color word. Strangely enough, his picture of his pastor is so clear that he is sure his pastor is really doing nothing. His *being* is his *doing*, so most people think, but that is not so.

One minister had been up for most of three nights and was eating an early breakfast in a local restaurant. He nearly dropped his coffee cup when the typical early morning group gathered for their coffee and one of them said for all to hear, "What's the preacher doing out this early? Preachers don't have to get up!" This is such a well-known phrase that most readers will not find it difficult to supply at least a dozen such situations from their own experience. Such ideas come from church officers; they would not be so disheartening if they came from non-Christians. Certainly they come from a complete lack of definition of the pastoral office.

Who can straighten both pastor and people out? The answer is not easy. The endless frustration resulting from the fact that people are unaware of the pastor's labors and are not cognizant of his role is merciless in its pressure. The people have never had a job description given to them as to the pastoral role. One layman who worked all of his adult life in church and who "grew up with preachers" stated rather categorically, "I think that a pastor is to preach, win the lost and visit the sick, and this he can do in no time if he works at it." He was saying that the pastor has more time on his hands than anyone.

Certainly his people witness his working two hours on Sunday and as one wag noted, he is the highest hourly wage earner in the community. Calling on a few sick people shouldn't take much time. The evangelistic house call is brief because the pastor is a professional "soul winner" who should produce like a salesman of any other product who is adept at selling his wares. Certainly if the list of baptisms and new converts is not up in number from previous years most laymen are convinced that the pastor is not good in this field. If he does not utilize his mental telepathic powers and guess about Aunt Sarah's partial stroke he is failing there. If the sermon is dull the following Sunday the average layman is quite convinced that his pastor has completely wasted the previous week. Thus, the pastor has obviously failed in the three principal areas of his duties—his duties as generally viewed, that is.

The endless moments of pressure exerted on him by the very fact that his people do not understand his role is a very realistic horror for the pastor. Who is this man called the local pastor? What is he doing with his time? The answers are many and most confusing. It is as Abraham Lincoln once said, "If we could first know where we were, and whither we are tending, we could better judge what to do, and how to do it."

Next there is the frustration caused by former pastoral relationships, in which some of his people have been intimate with a pastor previously known or have had friendships with pastors of other denominations who felt free to talk with them. A pastor has "let his hair down" around them and this gives them the right to say with a half smile that they really understand the enigma of this role because they have been on the inside with one pastor. This type of person walks in to a new pastor and boldly states that he or she is to call him by his first name and desires the same in return. He promises to be a close friend with the new pastor because of his personal acquaintance with another. Now if the relationship is not continued on this basis and if the pastor doesn't perform his duties as the former pastor did, this "new friend" has been known to become most vicious.

For instance, suppose for some reason the new pastor and his would-be "friend" cannot be close. This being the case, the layman gets his feelings hurt, and, it must be said, his pride hurt because the new pastor is not identifying with him as the former pastor did. Sometimes the closest friends of a former pastor can become the worst enemies of the present pastor. Some pastors have to live under the shadow of a previous pastor because the people will work hard at keeping the former man's memory and methods before the congregation.

There is confusion resulting from the dearth of historical material regarding the ministry of other men. So few men's biographies are helpful because most tend toward revealing the men on their summits. Most pastors have been known for their preaching and this side of their ministry is about all that is revealed. The *names* of great pastors of history are unimportant; indeed, many unknown to most laymen. Their moments of frustration and their moments of agony over the very things we have been saying have escaped the legacy of the pen. A few souls have hinted at this but have not been specific. This is natural because most autobiographies are written late in life and the past with its perils is easily overlooked. A real wild-fire becomes a tiny flame to the man who is twenty-five years removed from the heat. The greats of yesteryear were great preachers and builders of institutions, but how they handled the flesh and blood situations of the pastorate is amazingly lacking in their memoirs. That narrow escape when in the smaller church they "locked horns" and just barely survived is not mentioned in the autobiographical sketch.

Perhaps the omission is because the incident is too personal or because someone may yet be living who is either kin to the person in question or too close to the situation. Whatever the reason, the young pastor does not get to profit from these things because the older men will not write about them. Maybe this is one of history's greatest injustices to truth, that men in every profession tend to forget rainy days. These experiences have more than likely made men great far more than have their sermons.

One example of strength in crisis that has helped many a man is that of John writing of the church "boss" Diotrephes in his third letter. This vigorous stand has proved a great source of comfort to many men in similar situations and surely Diotrephes' kinfolks wouldn't have found it too complimentary of him had they read the letter. John's love for pre-eminence in the church caused the great apostle to take a strong and vigorous stand for truth. Many such situations have taken place but most men leave these out of their memoirs.

This dishonesty in not describing one's "downs" as well as "ups" hurts the younger pastors who sometimes get to thinking that the "greats" never had the same problems. The truth of the matter is that men are successful because they overcame the typical parish difficulties. It is a part of the best of us to try to forget our bad days. Maybe this is the reason for the absence of detail on this matter. For whatever reasons there may be, the pages devoted to the pastor's duties or other experiences are filled with the "glowing work," whereas the sordid, distasteful, crisis-filled moments of church problems are sometimes ignored completely. There is little help from recent or ancient history on the honest struggles of the pastor, but better and more honest biographies and autobiographies are being written all the time.

Few autobiographies tell of the days of near mental breakdown and the press of the people on the man. In this same vein, the older pastor ought to tell the younger man of his troubles. He should tell him that most of the time he will have to do as his Lord demanded and be "wise as serpents, and harmless as doves" (Matthew 10:16). No one ever understands that unless he is connected with lay people in an intimate capacity. Too many men have reversed it. Being wiser than a silly dove they have been shot out of the sky—great was their fall.

It is also a frustration to realize that sometimes people could be merely tolerating the pastor. He is thought by many to be a carry-over from another day. What pastor of late has not gone to a home in a grief situation and been treated by the younger sophisticates with a coldness and aloofness that borders on suspicion. It is as if he is a man out of another century who has to come and tell the people that "God's will has been done," offer a brief prayer and then leave. He is a comfort to the older people, but the younger set find in him a necessary evil they think time will finally eradicate.

That this present social order tolerates the pastor is further seen in its extolling of the roles of teachers in denominational schools and of denominational workers because they do not smack of the carry-over of the "parson" image. Even the missionaries are not to be called such but are to be called "teachers" in mission schools. Anything that hints of the "parson" image is greatly disparaged and it must be said that the pastor cannot escape this image because he is caught and he has no place to go. Therefore, he is tolerated today and is thought of as an intruder from another age and another world.

He is in the way most of the time, especially when his presence is not expected. The mad shuffle to hide the high-ball glasses and other indications of lighter moments is a scene of mass confusion if it is observed that the pastor is ringing the doorbell. He is really thought of as an intruder where most men are concerned, yet he is needed to bring moral guidance to the children and to aid the old folks in distress. As far as the mainstream of living is concerned, he is unwelcome and unwanted. This is his fault in a lot of cases, but there are some wonderful exceptions where some men have made genuine inroads of influence in the everyday lives of men and women. The present culture is controlled as much by church people as by non-church people.

The frustrations of the pastor are further compounded by his suffering from his own conscienciousness. Most men in the pastorate are deeply sincere about their place in this work, and can attest to some particular experience of deep commitment. It might have been an experience of a mystical nature or one that utilized much thought and rational behavior, not that the mystical is not rational, it is more spontaneous.

Regardless of the process that brings men into this work it can be said of most that they are in it for deeply dedi-cated reasons. Certainly the common conception that "most preachers are in it for money" is a carry-over of ignorance that defies human description.

The pastoral calling is bedrock to the New Testament. It is at the heart of the church and that makes it even more difficult because as the church is in revolution so will the pastor's office come under great stress. Most pastors are deeply in need of ways to fulfill their mission in the midst of such change. They want to be pleasing to God and they would like to be able to go home at the end of the day and know that they have not failed. Tangible evidence is so sparse that they can point to very little when day is done, and a thousand questions come to the mind of each man.

Did he say the right words in the counseling session? Did he pray the right prayer for the sick? Is he getting at the heart of the needs of his people in the Sunday sermons? Who is sick and in need of his care and expects him to know of it through extrasensory perception? Why was that particular man gruff to him in saying, "I haven't seen you lately. Aren't you seeing people any more?" or "I didn't get much out of your sermon last Sunday, Pastor." This adds the pressure of preparation against failure for the next Sunday and on and on until the pressure is unbearable to many. With a job that lacks so very much in concrete definition and where existing images are many, what man can be sure at sunset that he has fulfilled *any part* of his duties?

Some pastors have become so overly sensitive that they spend Sunday afternoon trying to figure out the complex attitudes of the people at the front door post-sermon greeting. Some were obviously peeved at the pastor's words and they will show it by their gruffness; others will have missed the point completely and they exhibit this by some inane statement. After a typical post-sermon greeting some pastors have felt so defeated they have developed the practice of seeing as few parishioners as possible after the sermon as a defense mechanism. The conscientious pastor is burdened with a guilt-ridden complex formed by constant self-questioning. Is he helping his people, or not? Is he pleasing to God? Is he fulfilling his calling? Sometimes that which would help his people might be his undoing, and words he should say he dares not say for fear the "pulpit will be declared vacant," as one old way of doing things declares.

Perhaps the greatest disillusionment comes from the thundering realization that the pastorate is not what the young aspirant thought it would be. There is no balloon that bursts any louder than when the young pastor gets into his first "full-time" situation. He has heard of the first year as a "honeymoon" and now knows what is subtly meant by "what happens after the honeymoon is over." The shock is too much for some tenderhearted souls. Who has not heard the statement, "If I knew that this was what I was getting into, I would have prepared myself in another area."

The subject of preparation brings us to a great flaw in the garment, the one of seminary preparation. The seminaries must tell the young student of the power structures he will encounter, of the harsh criticism to any sermon that makes people think, of the denominational pressure toward conformity, of the harassment by cliques, of the discontentment with a pastor that surfaces after a few years. They must equip him to handle criticism and to spot the most deadly of games people play—self-righteousness.

Some seminaries are no more than preacher factories and are controlled by their denominations. An atmosphere of sheer fright pervades many faculties. As a result, the student is on the losing end and does not get to witness the freedom of the best of intensive investigation. To the credit of most professors, they would want it to be different. However, many teachers of young pastors in seminaries today are men who have never been pastor of a church beyond that of a student ministry. They were hand-picked by an older professor and were given birth on their assignment not from the fires of actual experience but from the incubation of their school. This is not true of all the teachers; some have been in the pastorate, but for the most part most teachers wouldn't go back to the pastorate for all the "discounts" in the world.

As once "successful pastors who now teach," they sometimes fail to inform the young student. Someone ought to tell him that his greatest enemies may be men on his board and his best friends may be those who are not active within the institutional church. He has been led to believe that evil is in the liquor industry and in the vicious elements of indifference. Although evil is in these areas, no one tells him that the most entrenched evil he is to endure could come from his new church's leading members. The young pastor is seized with terror when his job is threatened either openly or in a thousand devious ways. As one president of a missionary society bluntly stated to a new pastor, "I can get your job."

Who has prepared the young aspirant for this? Certainly many seminaries do not. He is greatly frustrated when he realizes that his professors have left a lot unsaid about church life. However, there are some very courageous professors who are trying to come to the aid of the pastorate.

No discussion of the pastor's pressures is complete without mention of the one of winning converts. This personal duty of being an ambassador of the gospel is weighty and it is a shock to learn that most of this weight is on his shoulders. He is the connecting link with the unchurched man. It is too obvious for words that the enlistment of new converts is a pressure squarely on the shoulders of the pastor. The pressure is freighted further by the denomination on the one side and the congregation on the other.

Basically most pastors have such a sincere love of souls that they want to do this God-given work. Winning new converts comes hard and the job is even harder when denominational workers and the pastor's own people put him in a pincer movement to produce. He is further shocked to find that some of the converts of former pastors are no longer in attendance or to any degree active. Sometimes his time is spent trying to reconvert the converted.

Another incitement to the frustration of the pastor is that he suffers from the social expectation of excellence, yet he is spread too thin to be excellent in any one area. Many pastors preach twice on Sunday and speak to a group on Wednesday night. It can be said with practical accuracy that none of the greats often quoted from the pulpit could have been great preachers if they had had to produce that often. Most of the greats or near-greats preached only once on Sunday and some of them were off for at least two months in the summers.

It is not fair to impose upon a man the responsibility of this many sermons. He learns to do what few others in our society do: give his second-best because there is just not sufficient time to do more. This adjustment is a terrible psychological blow to his sermon preparation and causes a guilt complex known only to the pure at heart. The limitation is further aggravated when a visitor from a seminary or college, or a denominational officer, comes and preaches to the gallery. The people are sure their pastor is not studying or he would deliver sermons equally polished and brilliant every Sunday. When denominational workers sell their wares, as they usually do, the people are certain that their pastor is not "mission-minded." How else can one explain that the pastor is not as enthusiastic as the denominational drummer?

Most pastors have discovered that living over the effects

of the mass hypnotic spell of the evangelist is a real crisis. The people can't understand why the pastor is so "dull" and why he does not preach with "power." He *cannot* be an excellent preacher with the number of sermons he has to produce. Yet, unconsciously, the people compare him with the excellence of other men in the pulpit. Their reaction to the pastor's preaching is most different from their reaction to the preaching of a visitor. The pastor as preacher cannot possibly excel each time; giving three sermons a week, he wonders if he can excel at *any* time.

The pastor as counselor defies excellence because he cannot give himself to preparation for this pursuit. To be ready to counsel several hundred members in all kinds of situations scares the average pastor to death. He is to counsel family problem situations, teen-age delinquency and old-age boredom, and he can jump from one to the other in less time than it takes to open a door. The fear of hurting a situation instead of helping it, is a real frustration to an intelligent pastor.

Our society is one of excellence in many areas. The television repairman now tells you whether he specializes in black and white models or in color sets. He even has a charge for a house call and a different one for an office call. Every form of our life is one of producing excellence in service to people or one doesn't last long.

One pastor tells of a Sunday morning episode that is not farfetched by any means. At half past nine he taught a young adult Sunday school class. From there he rushed into the pulpit to preach. After the sermon the board called a special meeting at which he led a discussion of the immediate need for a ten-thousand dollar loan for new air-conditioning equipment. While he was in this discussion the phone rang. The caller was the local funeral director who said that a man had been torn apart in a tractor accident and that his wife thought him still alive and was in the waiting room of a hospital instead of the waiting room of a funeral home. The funeral director wanted the pastor to tell her that her husband was dead. The pastor rushed over and dealt as best as he could with the grief situation. He was sick all afternoon from exhaustion but had to preach again that night.

Is there any wonder that men are leaving the pastorate in record numbers? More would leave if they were prepared to do anything else and still satisfy some aspect of what they consider their call.

The pastor is under great stress in that he is to be the prime example of what he preaches on Sunday. This also includes his family. He, unlike visiting preachers who come and go, has to stay under the gaze of his people. The sincere pastor is most zealous in practicing what he preaches; however, he preaches so much that he sometimes forgets what he said and when he last said it. He is in the position of having to say so much that he says very little, which is obvious to all. Before long he has said all he knows and lived all he knows and the brook is dry. He yearns for another situation and for the opportunity to preach his store to new people. This very cycle becomes vicious, and when it dawns on any tenderhearted soul that this will be his fare until retirement he awakens like a caged animal and the pacing starts in his heart. He knows that the people will soon tire of him and as he looks at his older pastor friends he realizes that the average pastor starts downhill at about the same age the professional man in any other occupation begins to enjoy the fruits of his labors.

No man likes the assessment that he is only average, but a little voice tells him that he is *not* a cut above most men, so he has very little to look forward to. Every man looks forward to retirement as the crowning years of his labors, but not so with the pastor. He is amazingly expendable in those years when other men are producing most. Most business pursuits want the inspiration of years of experience but this is pathetically unlike the church. Church people want the inspiration of the moment and a young man with a flair for the dramatic and an appeal in preaching can unseat an older man with wisdom in most situations. The older man is said to have lost his "fire," though he may just be properly prepared to really serve people.

Very probably at the heart of the frustration for the dedicated, sincere pastor is that his job never ceases. Now this does not mean that he is to be pitied. It is simply that there is never a day when by closing his study door is he free from the gnawing thought of that other book he should read to help him and his people. There is the faint voice that asks if he has not failed to make the proper call on the home that needed him so badly. What seeking soul was yearning for an ambassador of the gospel to tell him of deliverance from his bondage? He knows that he could do a little more with the sermons for the next Lord's Day. Can he come up with something to help his people? This follows him to recreation and everywhere else he goes. People have a way of not letting a man forget that he is their pastor, even in his time off. Constantly, "shop talk" about the church is the conversation. Ultimately his health is affected because of the ceaseless duration of the strain.

These are not all of the frustrations of the modern pastor's predicament. These are only a very few, yet any one of these is capable of breaking an average man in any other job. All of this has to do basically with his image. It can be said very frankly that the pastor's image as it is viewed is getting close to the heart of the problem of the restlessness of the modern pastor whether he be young or old. He is truly in a goldfish bowl and, like a goldfish, he is usually forced into going in circles by his frustrations.

2

The Many Images of the Man

The Church directed my life into some channels I had not foreseen, but it has not lessened my enthusiasm for the Christian ministry.—GERALD H. KENNEDY

Some time ago the President of the United States was worshiping in a church on Sunday morning when the preacher of the hour asked him most pointedly in a rhetorical manner about America's involvement in Vietnam. A heated controversy followed that is a positive picture of the thesis of this chapter.

The minister was deluged with mail, as we would expect. Whether he was right or wrong is not important. The significant thing is that thousands of criticisms or sentiments, reaching even into the halls of Congress, can be summed up in a line men have heard since they can remember. It starts out "I don't think a preacher has any business. . . ."

This is a fascinating illustration of the fact that though a man occupies the position of pastor he is one of the most limited individuals in the community. There are many bars to his private prison. Each bar is represented by "I don't think a preacher should. . . ." Now this sentence can be completed with such words as "do," "say," "go," "think," "be," "get" and just about any other description of an action there is because each bar represents an image.

When Paul said he was becoming all things to all men he certainly didn't mean that the pastorate had no solidarity in conceptual lines. All too often the pastoral role has sadly developed into "all things to all men." It is whatever laymen think a pastor should say, do, or think, or however act, that is the image these laymen demand before a man fulfills himself in their eyes. They do not stop to ask themselves how they came to the conclusions they register on the life of this man in the pastoral office. For instance, in the field of politics a doctor, teacher, lawyer, engineer and others will get involved and most people will praise them for their unselfishness and their interest in good government, but a minister need merely voice an opinion and is quickly told that "pastors are to stay out of politics." Where did this image of pastoral non-involvement come from? There could be answers in the social development of the pastorate through history but answers to the questions are not as important for these purposes as is the need to show *that there are horrible strangle holds* on a pastor and that they *do exist.*

The frustrations of the pastors have led to the predicament of the pastoral ranks. Who of us has not witnessed the headlong rush to leave the pastoral ministry? A great number of men leave the pastorate each year and these are men with various degrees of training, many of them being divinity school graduates. Denominational jobs are rapidly sought after and in many cases these positions are created for men who have been in influential positions as pastors. Laymen have asked why some denominational scaffolding is being enlarged and what is being built. One answer is the old story of bureaucracy, the extension of the machine to create positions in order to provide jobs.

Just who are these jobs for? They are for pastors who consciously or unconsciously want to get out of the pastorate. It may shock some laymen to observe that one answer to their question is this one of *getting away from the pastorate.* The pay is better, the security and benefits are better and these men are removed from the day-to-day problems of the pastorate. Who has known of any number of these men *going back into the pastorate?* This is not to decry denominational structures but only to point out some truths that are known but not often stated for public consumption.

A good many pastors are going into teaching positions. Here again there are not enough places for the men to go after that first heartbreaking pastorate and as is the case with many, after two or three pastorates all tragically alike. That we are losing men is a fact worth repeating. What is the trouble? Laymen who are sincerely interested are seriously asking this question. Can something be done about it? Perhaps getting it into the open will help some, but a good many books will have to be printed and digested before we can come to any hopeful solution and then pray that it is not too late for the quality of men we desire in the pastorate.

There is an almost hostile attitude toward the pastorate on the part of many pastors. Elton Trueblood, writing on the problem of pastors says, "They may not be entirely clear about the image of the ministry which would be acceptable to them, but they are very clear about what it is which they hate." The problem is not objection to what they consider the real work they are called to do, but a *hatred for the peripheral* and for the *image* they have inherited. This is felt keenly when a pastor is introduced to a stranger and is immediately thrown into the role of a listener to the latest "preacher joke," which is usually inane. Many pastors hide their feelings quite well before their congregations, but things are different at convention time with their fellows. If laymen could hear the typical sessions of convening pastors, it would probably cure our problems overnight or completely deplete the ranks. At these times, church switching and political maneuvering for another congregation is as typical as eating.

In an earlier discussion of the pastor's frustrations it was posited that the greatest burden his office carries is the lack of definitive outline in the New Testament. Perhaps since the days of canonized Scripture and surely since the days of the availability of the Bible to laymen, the office has been left to interpretation on the part of any reader of the documents. As has been said, they cover adequately what he is to be in conduct but as to his duties there are few specifications. So at this point the door is left open to the interpretations of that lofty office that have been forced on many good men and that literally shortened their days. Some of these images become hindrances to a man and his work because all too often they regulate his activities and make a slave of him so that he is not prepared to be a father, husband *or* preacher. Like the fingers touching a goldfish bowl they cause the poor creature to jump and turn in all directions until he has lost his sense of direction and bearing.

Any discussion of his role as a man of many images has to begin with the era when the pastor was perhaps the most influential man in the community. When this started is uncertain and unimportant. The important truth is that it no longer exists today and he is not the most influential man in the community. Surely the day of his great influence was never more marked than during what we know as the age of Victorian ethics. The pastor was the interpreter of these ethics and basically it was he who molded the ideas for the consumption of the community at large.

To say that there is a real rebellion against the standards and ethics of another day is to put it too mildly. This generation for the most part does not want anything to do with any vestige of a carry-over from that day. Its image of the local pastor is that of a man out of step, a creature sadly out of tune with present-day thought. It must be said with all honesty that this *is* the case with many pastors who are completely incapable of dealing with the problems of today's world but it is not so with all pastors. When one self-styled minister makes a speech at the Ku Klux Klan rally, it damages the image of all the other ministers overnight.

The idea that the pastor has nothing positive to offer is illustrated by an incident that happened to one minister when a small child died. When he walked into the home, the distraught father said, "All right, Reverend, I'm glad you are here, but I don't want any pious platitudes at a time like this." He really didn't think that the pastor had anything worthwhile to say to him. Another man actually said to his pastor that his services were good and much needed for his parents, who were in a rest home, but that he himself didn't have any time for religion. This is an age of rebellion as never before, and the rebellion against the church is basically *a rebellion against the pastor.* He is seen as the chief caretaker of antiquities.

Perhaps the idea that he is irrelevant stems from fact; that is to say, the pastor's image *has been* at times one of irrelevance. One current idea is that the pastor is not really a flesh and blood individual. He is looked upon as a creature without feeling. He is to live perfectly, respond to every situation with the highest degree of Christian living and when he doesn't, he is more severely criticized than any other man in the community. In fact, grounds for dismissal of a pastor can start with as little as a rude word to the most influential person in the congregation. His mistakes are looked for and sometimes anticipated and this also applies to his wife. Her role would merit several books on the general subject of the images women have of her. The pastor is to minister to everyone else and to their children and this sometimes means an infringement on the time spent with his own family. Consequently his own vineyard grows up in weeds while he works another's. The stories of ministers' children going astray are legion, although they are greatly overdone.

The pastor's own spiritual needs are hardly noticed by the congregation. He has no pastor for the most part. Some denominations overcome this by a highly structured ecclesiastical organization, but in reality the men of those churches are just as "pastorless." To have a bishop in the capital city is some help, but these bishops have so many men under them that they cannot offer the kind of everyday help the parish pastor must have. Everyone else in the congregation has a person to counsel with and one to admonish and provide inspiration on Sunday, but the pastor's well runs dry so often. There is the mistaken idea that he does not need the strength he gives to others. He is never thought to doubt or have moments of deep depression when his own world, like everyone else's, has to be put back together. He is more like a bloodless being free of sin, a visitant from the land of no temptations. On the other hand, a few recent books and movies have been made on the subject of a minister's sin; these have done the pastoral role as great an injustice as the idea that he is almost sinless. Hawthorne's *The Scarlet Letter* is a most poignant and meaningful description of a minister's weaknesses. It is done with taste and preserves the man and his office.

Another image held by many, and surely a carry-over of another day, is that the pastor is primarily a social worker. There was a day when the churches were smaller and centered in a close-knit community setting, but now things are different. In many sections the small country church is gone and the concentration of people is in larger towns. Sadly enough, many of the present generation of church members remember those days before World War II when the preacher made a call on each family every week or so. People did not expect as much from him then, and modes of transportation, like life itself, went at a generally slower pace. It would help a lot if people could *forget those days* because they no longer exist. Today the pastor drives a good car and he is expected to come and visit often. Exactly what he is supposed to do when he arrives at a home is uncertain. Basically, he is to spend a bit of time talking about almost anything.

This idea of his expected visit is the worst problem of the pastor with people over fifty-five years. Their image of his role was crystallized a long time ago by "ol' Parson Jones" back where they came from. As some of these people near retirement, they have more time on their hands and their conception of the pastor is one of a man who has time, time and more time. They sit and run out of something to do and then it strikes them that they would like to see the pastor. He would make good company and they can remember when Reverend and Mrs. Jones used to call on their folks and stay much of the afternoon. The sight of the reverend and his wife calling was a familiar one in days gone by, and this image is still rigidly imposed on many pastors today. These people are sure that the pastor doesn't have anything to do but prepare a brief outline, which he delivers any way but briefly, and then is free several days of the week.

Now if there is news of a death or a wedding, people are most patient and quick to say that they know the pastor is busy but aside from these events he is free to "go calling." This ultimately will lead to a fight for his time and, more importantly, his attention. What young pastor has not visited in a community to be severely rebuked the following Sunday by neighbors who remark that they saw him visiting at such and such a place and they waited for him to come over to their house but he didn't. They may assume that he just doesn't care for them, or that their home isn't good enough. Basically people sometimes want the attention and identification with the pastor's visit *more* than the joy of having the man as a person in their homes.

Social calling is an expected part of the routine of the duties of a pastor, but in our present fast-paced world a man would have a terrible problem finding people at home even if he did have the time. It takes a lot of planning, effort and time to leave an office and stop what one is doing in order to go to a home, and it is a real adjustment to find these people out. Perhaps he will not have another such free moment in a week. People forget this and wonder why he can't come over, say the next afternoon. What pastor hasn't had the experience of being severely criticized for not visiting the shut-ins, only to find that the people in question are fishing when he does go to their home? Somehow they can't go to church, but they vehemently demand that the church be brought to them.

Those who are the most involved in the life of a church demand the least from the pastor. Because only a very small percentage of any membership is actively engaged in the work of the church, it is easy to see where the point of stress is located. There is a large percentage of each church that demands the most from a pastor. When one of their loved ones dies, they want a choir and the full complement of voices, time by the hour from the pastor and leaders of the church and any other service tradition has rendered. This need for attention does not stop with the funeral but is fully expected periodically afterward.

The hail-fellow-well-met back slapper image of the pastor is one of the most offensive. However, if the pastor doesn't come into the business establishments of his people then they may ask where he has been and what he has been doing. Why haven't they seen him for some time? In some localities the business end of life takes on a higher meaning when the pastor comes by, and it is always good for street talk to include the news that the pastor "was in just a day or two ago." Some ministers go up one side and down the other side of the street sticking their heads in the door of each place of business in order to just say, "Hi," a trip that could take an hour each day.

Of course this type of glad-hander is also criticized for not having anything to do but walk the streets. He is seen drinking coffee several times a day and is usually branded as a loafer but a jolly good fellow because he is good at talking about hounds, hunting, fishing and golf. Now if he is not on the street and if he does not frequent the coffee shop, he is accused of being too much to himself and not a good mixer.

This term "good mixer" is very fascinating. There have been many pastors who have lost their jobs over this one void in their personality. One wonders if the pastor's main function is not "to mix." That could just about cover the whole campground because the image of the good mixer is an absolute must for the successful pastor. Now this automatically rules out the retiring in spirit or the naturally shy person. It makes no difference whether he is a good counselor or thinker, if he is not a "good mixer" he is taboo. It is easier for a pastor to follow a good pulpit man than a good mixer, that is, if one is just a mediocre mixer. His people will curse him on Sunday for poor preaching but praise him Monday through Saturday for good mixing.

There ought to be a course in every seminary on mixing. Each church has cliques and to offend one is to offend several people. Nevertheless he has to learn to mix with all of them.

Closely akin to his social calling is something that is most legitimate but grossly over-expected, that is "shut-in" calling. First of all, there needs to be a correct definition of who is a shut-in. Just because a person is past retirement doesn't qualify him for a shut-in. Also a physical disability such as fallen arches, slight deafness and many other "critical" illnesses does not merit a systematic visit from the pastor. This is the day of the convalescent home and many older people live in these homes much like hotels. Their sons and daughters place them there for various and good reasons. Many times these sons and daughters have guilt complexes about not visiting as much as they should. They call their pastor's office and ask if he wouldn't make calls on lonely mother or dad. The pastor, of course, has the necessary time to sit with them and this soothes the needs quite well for both the shut-in *and* the son or daughter. There are some real cases of shut-ins; these are people who truly can't get out, and most pastors are more than happy to call on these dear people and do as time permits.

It is a normal thing to get a phone call at least once a week to the effect that someone has been saying around town that the pastor has not called. The caller is informing the pastor so that in his spare time, as the caller puts it, he can go. Once a week for a year makes a fairly large number of malcontents to call on. Or there is the good woman or man who comes in to tell the pastor that he has had "Uncle Joe" on his heart and he just wanted the pastor to drop by and cheer the old fellow up. After all, the pastor is to jump when a member says something is "on his heart." This makes it almost a divine revelation, but one can eat too much and have a "heavy heart" as well. However, the laymen have learned this language from the "on my heart" pastors who have used this gimmick to get their way.

One pastor tells of an experience so cutting that it must be told for lay reader consumption. It seems that he followed a very poor preacher and the congregation had just about gone to the baker's dozen. However, this good man was constantly on the run visiting this one and that and jumping at every beck and call. Our pastor friend who followed such a routine was getting criticism. He applied himself diligently to study and thorough preparation for the arduous task of preaching three times a week. The day before the incident in question he received a call from a hospital seventy-five miles away. A schoolteacher's wife had lost a baby in birth. She was fraught with anxiety and needed someone to reassure her. Both she and her husband were members of another denomination from that of this pastor. Since the schoolteacher's pastor was out of the state, he called on this man. There were other churches of his denomination back in his town and other pastors available, but he crossed denominational lines because he had heard that this pastor was a good thinker and one who could speak for God. The good pastor dropped his business at hand and motored to the city to offer strength to the bereaved woman.

The next day he was busy preparing a graveside service for the still-born infant. He was about ready to go to the cemetery when a lady walked into his office and asked for a moment of his time. He recognized her as the wife of one of his members although she was a member of another church and, strangely enough, it was the same church of the grief-stricken parents. He thought she might be bringing a good word of commendation for the work he was doing while her own pastor was away. He was completely shocked when this lady said she had come to help his reputation.

It seems that she lived in a neighborhood of his members and one old gentleman was busy about the neighborhood complaining that the new pastor had only visited his home twice in the past year and that he didn't care for people as the last pastor had. "He didn't care." "He didn't care." These words cut like a knife. The pastor bluntly excused the lady, remarking that if these people had any complaints they could come themselves. This man had over one thousand resident members and was in the process of offering hope to people of another congregation in town. Now, it is demands like this that are quickly depleting the pastoral ranks. There can be no ministry that anyone could possibly deem as Christian in a setting of back-slapping, house-calling idleness.

Any mention of the word "change" brings up another image the layman has of his pastor. He is transient! And how he is transient! Many laymen like the idea greatly and so do many pastors. This means that underneath it all there is the thin level of lack of permanency to all that he does. He is ever reminded that the church has done it such and such a way for as long as people can remember and that pastors have come and gone—*emphasis on gone*—and he had better adjust to it. As one man said, "Come weal or woe, my status is quo."

This is also reflected in the idea people present to him in the statement, "You better get used to us." After one naive young pastor offered to change a phase of the church organization, one church official read him the riot act. Of course, had the pastor talked this way to the official, he would have had to pack up and go. After the confrontation a friendly sort of fellow ambled up to him and said, "Pastor, Joe didn't mean anything, he chews all our pastors out. You will have to get used to him."

Common sense dictates that it is easier for several hundred people to adjust to the personality of one man than for one man, namely the pastor, to have to adjust to the idiosyncrasies of all the congregation, but that isn't the way it works. The assumption that a pastor will not be long in the same pulpit thwarts some effort in praying for him and attempting to aid his plans for the church. No one will come to the aid of the pastor if he has a quirk of personality, but the congregation, often to the last man, *demands* that the pastor understand it because, after all, he is transient and will not always be there.

This idea of the "transient" means that many people who might love the pastor genuinely will not do so because no sooner would they come to love him than he would move on. So they have determined never again to be close to another pastor. Furthermore, problems that arise and which might break communication lines are tolerated without any effort toward resolution.

Some church governments give rise to the most unhealthy attitude of he-works-for-us-image. This is a sordid perversion and a critical problem. In one small parish a recent seminary graduate with the equivalent of a medical practitioner's education was told by his board that the grass on the church property was tall and needed mowing. The young pastor was not an exceptional pulpit man, which in that particular area meant that he didn't holler loud or long enough and that he did not know he was to mow the church lawn adjoining the parsonage property. As his friends jokingly said of him, he was told to mow or go. He soon got another call to what was hoped to be a truly Christian congregation.

The idea of the "owned man" or the "kept man" is portrayed visibly within the parsonage itself, for the parsonage often reminds the pastor of a kind of patronage. To be furnished a house has implications that a house allowance, which is much better, does not have. It is really not his house and he is made constantly aware of it. In the smaller communities, what pastor has not experienced people coming in to use the rest rooms or to get a drink of water early Sunday morning? And how many stars in the crown of many a dear pastor's wife have been put there by the idea of a parsonage? If the church pays the utilities, then the lights had better be off and the doors closed. Most parsonages are repaired beautifully, right after they have nearly fallen apart, and that condition sometimes exists through three or four pastors' tenures. Some parsonages never would get adequately repaired if the church were not trying to get some new "cracker-jack" preacher who, after one look at the house, would have demanded the needed repairs. If the parsonage is better than the average home, it serves as a constant reminder that the pastor lives in a "palace" while his people live in houses of "mud and straw."

For those men who deal with pulpit committees, there is a new world in every visit. They must invariably ask if the committee represents the thinking of the church. The answer is always "yes," whether this is true or not. One of the visiting committee members will always ask about the *pastor's program,* which means, How does he put on the "rousements"? They *know* that he preaches, teaches, visits, etc., but they always ask about his "program." Does he have new gimmicks for growth? Could he possibly have the keys to the Kingdom? They are heard to say, "If we can find the right man, our situation will really go!" Of course, with this philosophy underlying the call of the church, if the church doesn't "really go" in a certain number of months it doesn't take a really intelligent person to figure out what's wrong: they have the *wrong* man. So, the pastor becomes expendable.

A very good illustration occurred in a rapidly growing suburban area where a church became pastorless. A committee called on a pastor to inquire of his readiness to accept their offer, and he was about ready to agree to the challenge when the chairman of the committee said, "Within a year our church will double its size and budget. All a man has to do is open the doors of the church and we will have members." The pastor caught this remark and declined the offer. He warned the men that their attitude was commercial and dangerous. He told them they were treating the situation as a university would in hiring a football coach and bribing him with a new stadium of a great capacity. He told them that they were forcing the image of a recruiter on their pastoral office and, as would an unsuccessful coach, the next pastor would have to go within a year if he *did not produce.* The committee left in a huff.

The minister zealously followed the work of that committee when they called a young man right out of the seminary. Within a year the young pastor had resigned to go back to the seminary and do postgraduate work. This came as no surprise. It is the "out" for many men. A check of the statistics determined that the church had had a ten percent gain and a neighboring church a thirty percent gain. The pastor was doing a fine job but he was not the spectacular image the church needed to attract people. It is significant that the church had not grown at all as the committee had expected. The cult of numbers includes laymen as well as pastors and this image the layman has of the great promoter and "program man" is perilously close to paganism. Many pastors are indoctrinated by denominational boards and agencies to produce greater numbers than their churches have done before. A business concern checks its work by the year before to the day. Business men make up the churches and when this "a year ago" attitude is the criterion for judging success it pressures many a pastor into "post-graduate work."

In these days of church growth, people have become accustomed to talking about church statistics. Additions to the church are regularly printed in church bulletins, and this has made the members conscious of the pastor's leadership. (Perhaps this was the purpose all along.) "Since I came" is a familiar phrase. When the visible evidences of growth begin to dwindle, the pastor is expected to leave. One of the things people say is, "He has been here long enough." At first, this is an idle statement; only later does it become a movement for him to leave since pastors are expected to produce in the statistic column.

People come very close to playing God when they say such things as "I don't think a pastor ought to stay over ———years." Once the idea prevails in the minds of enough people that the pastor is not producing, then his ministry is greatly hindered. Perhaps this would be a good place to inject the words of one far wiser than this writer when he warned young Timothy against "idle talk."

Who is to ultimately say when the shepherd has led his flock far enough? Surely good men have had their ministry cut short because of idle talk. Then there is the board member who is sure that what his church needs is the image of a younger man. This sounds good to most everyone in this day of the young executive. Young men in old settled churches have discovered that when they say something that resounds with the truth of years gone by, the people acclaim them to be older than their years and undoubtedly brilliant. However, let a man speak of a new approach, and the people will shake their heads and say patiently, "He is just young. He will know better when he gets older." People, though not meaning harm, can bring about severe crises in the life of a church. Many shepherds have been put out to pasture by elders who were convinced that if God didn't move the man they would, *and they did.* Surely the final day of judging will bring to light many other hidden reasons and personality conflicts that were passed off as "too long on the field."

Another such statement reflects the image that he must be well liked. It is, "How do you like the pastor?" This sounds like an innocent inquiry but leads itself to the most vicious of talk. How well a man is liked should not be the deciding factor in the appraisal of his work. After a certain stage in a particular Galilean preacher's life, the people followed Him no more and He ultimately lost His following, except for a few faithful women and one lone man. Certainly if His ministry were judged according to His popularity in those days, He would have failed. His work is seen in retrospect as having the most meaning in those dark days.

Seeking the approval of the masses is a poor pursuit, but many are in this pathway. When this is sensed by some laymen, the pastor is asking for an endless task of pleasing people and once this is started there is no stopping. Perhaps one way to please people is the image of the pastor who visits for every ill from a mashed finger to acute and serious illnesses. The pastor has a real ministry to the seriously ill, but he has no particular function as a Christian pastor in visiting people with the common cold. Where did the idea arise that the pastor was to be continually aware of the minor illnesses of his flock? It is here nevertheless and to the critically ill he owes much time and prayer. However, some pastors spend most of their time in hospital visitation, especially in cities. Some even make hospital calls as far as one hundred fifty miles away for just routine check-ups of the patient. When some ministers have tried in desperation to change this hospital visitor image they have been met with intense hostility and the threat of a personal Armageddon. The young Josiahs can fall quicker because of the failure to visit "Uncle Joe" than for any other reason.

There was a time when a hospital stay by a person was a thing of real seriousness but in this day of hospital insurance, people are found to go to the hospital for a rest. This is not distinguished by the average person and he wants the pastor to call every day. Besides, days are long in a hospital and since the pastor "doesn't have anything to do" he should make a lengthy visit to each person. This business of visiting the members just because they come under the general heading of sick is ridiculous.

First of all, it is dangerous to the pastor and to his family because he has no business in a room in which the patient has fever, of which the pastor is unaware because he doesn't have access to the hospital charts. He can expose himself to illnesses that can greatly impair his real ministry to his people or he can bring illnesses home to his family. Surely in this day of medical science the pastor is asking for serious trouble if he bounces in and out of hospital rooms. Many of his doctor friends tell him to stay away, but the family insists on his call. Is this a carry-over of superstition when the medicine man was also the witch doctor or the high priest? Some people believe that when the pastor prays and the doctor gives an injection, relief is soon on its way.

All too often the pastor is unaware of situations that require his presence and obviously many people think that the seminary must offer a course in mental telepathy. One pastor tells the story of being in a new church for about three weeks when his secretary was called and rather bluntly told that her boss was failing in his duties. A certain member had been in the hospital for four days and did not receive a visit. The pastor went to the office of the disgruntled person, who was back on the job the day after the hospital had dismissed her. He asked her why she was angry and she said that men from other churches had called on her but her pastor had not. Obviously her ego was hurt more than her acute sinusitis (from which the pastor suffered perennially). He very wisely asked her if she had called her doctor, knowing that she had. Then she volunteered that she had put her pet dog in the kennels for the three days. The pastor remarked that if she could call the doctor and the caretaker of her dogs, surely she could have called the shepherd of her soul—if it were that important to her. Needless to say he made a point—and an enemy.

Another image people have is the one of the pastor as the official offerer of prayer. He is to pray at many functions all the way from Little League baseball to the dedication of a new roof on the Legion hall. Most pastors do not relish this, but it is an expected and necessary part of their cultural image. This is not a big task and it is in keeping with what many laymen think of his role, that he is the official doer of the *necessary but innocuous routines of life.*

There needs to be something said about the image some laymen have of the pastor as a truant officer for church. If some member of the congregation misses church, he invariably asks, "Did you miss me Sunday?" If the pastor says "yes," sometimes he is a liar and if he says "no," he is accused of not caring. This ties in with the image that the pastor as preacher is supposed to "step on my toes." One man went out of church and remarked that the pastor really stepped on his toes in that sermon. The pastor said that he appreciated that sincere confession and asked if he were coming back to church that night, since he had preached on loyalty. The man said he would give it some thought; however, he did not come back. There was no correlation at all in the reaction of the individual and the truth of what the pastor had said, yet this man was representative of a group that demands that a pastor step on their toes, whatever that may mean. More will be said of this in a later chapter.

Some have suggested that this desire for bombastic preaching is really a way out for the individual and an escape from real Christian commitment. It is viewed as taking a man's conscience out and beating it publicly, then putting it back inside the man. This "washing of his sins" in public will do him for another week. Many men do not want a pastor who will make them think; that is the last thing they want to do. Someone has said, "Make a man think he is thinking and he will love you. Make him think and he will hate you."

Perhaps the greatest pressure in the form of images stems from the existing images each community has and which it forces on its new minister. These images become *dominant cultural patterns.* Illustrations of each peculiar situation are not meant for repetition but rather to serve as pictures of practical clarity, especially for the benefit of laymen who want to help.

In every pastoral situation there are images in the minds of the people as to the office. These images have been set or molded by many conditions previously existing. Past pastors, especially those whose tenure was long, have set ideas in motion as to the duties of the pastor in that particular locality. Paul Scherer hits at the heart of this when he warns that, "We are to fashion our own advantages. We are to create and cultivate our own tastes. We are to set our own lofty standards. We are to be the pioneers of our strain; not content with minimum requirements, with narrow outlooks, with inherited prejudices. Every effort must be made to broaden the horizons of life; to push out the boundaries of normal human experience; to extend our knowledge of literature, of language, of science, and of the arts: 'That the man of God may be perfect' (II Timothy 3:17)."

How much is the pastor to conform to the image set in the minds of his new church? Is he, in order to be a good pastor, to reflect the biases and prejudices of his congregation? It is interesting to note that after the Supreme Court decision concerning segregation, many pastors became involved pro and con in the debate. Pastors who had never preached a sermon for segregation or for integration now made headlines. It is truly interesting that some pastors became arch-segregationists in strong segregationist sections, and in strong integrationist sections pastors waxed long and loud for equality.

The image was set for these men as to what they were to say and many of them followed the mold. Some men courageously defied the image and are to be commended, not as much for what they said as for the fact that they were voices, not echoes. Local cultural images of the pastor's position are hard to change; however, the church is to redeem society, not give sanction to its ways. This is also true with the pastor. He is not to represent the mind of his community or even his church. He is to represent the mind of God to men. Samuel McCrea Cavert in a *Pulpit Digest* editorial entitled "For Whom Does the Pulpit Speak?" states, "The idea that 'the voice of the pulpit' should be only 'the voice of the congregation' is widely held but it is completely at variance with the viewpoint of the Bible."

We have talked about the back-slapper, now let us examine the great organizer. He is going to call a meeting and appoint a committee every time the denominational headquarters insists that he do so. He wants to keep in good with the leadership of his denomination so he responds favorably to all the mail he gets and he convinces his people that the "greatest" minds have suggested that they do such and so. Consequently, the church becomes a great machine. Of course, this type of person will not stay long in his church because his fidelity to the denomination will get him a larger parish in no time. *But the image is fixed in the minds of the people* and they are proud that their pastor "went up."

The new pastor is no sooner inside the front door of the pastorium than this image strikes him and people meet him and assure him that he is in the right place. "Our church sends men to larger ones" is the statement heard so often, with the new pastor being immediately informed that Reverend Smith had everything perfectly organized and all he will have to do is move in and start steering the machine. The image is fixed and even the men in the denominational headquarters look upon this church as a "strong" church, meaning, of course, that it is a strong field for denominational policies. The new pastor can take it no longer, so he raises his voice against the methods being forced upon him. To the amazement of some of his people, their image hasn't taken effect yet. In some cases, church people have been known to take a trip to the bishop or denominational headquarters to inform on the "heretical" tendencies of the new pastor.

The new pastor is in trouble if he follows the "constant visitor" image. As we have already mentioned, the pastors in "the good old days" spent many hours in homes. His contemporary equivalent will do the same thing. He will sit down for hours and chat with the older ladies. The women's missionary society loves him dearly and he of all people has generally been referred to as a "real" pastor. Sometimes his wife goes with him and people who are older love to see them come.

In every church there is a group of people who can well remember the day when pastors did this as part of their routine. It doesn't dawn on them that their church "back home" had fifty members and their present church has three hundred and fifty. They still want their pastor to drop by every week because somehow he "owes" it to them. It might be said that these people never drop in on him, but he still is to come by periodically.

When following a person like this, a younger man especially is in for some headaches. He will be met at the door every Sunday and reminded that Reverend Visitall came often whereas he never comes to see them. The truth is that Reverend Visitall never studied, but preached sermons written years ago. The people slept through his sermons but could excuse him because he was a "real" pastor. Some pastors succumb to this image and use it as an excuse to keep from diligent study. The young student right out of the seminary with his mind disciplined for study finds this type situation a "veritable Hell." Perhaps young boys have heard their parents discuss the pastor's inability to conform to the cultural image so much that they have determined not to enter the ministry for any reason.

Another image of the pastor is that of a "handy man." If the pastor is not careful, he will be called upon to make trips for members that have nothing to do with his calling as a minister, except that he was tagged with the handyman image when he accepted the church. One pastor tells of a woman, one of a congregation of sixteen hundred, who called him to ask to be taken to a doctor in a city fifty miles away. Her excuse was that she didn't want to take an earlier bus and have to wait two hours in the doctor's office and furthermore the previous pastor had taken her. The new pastor did not, but he lost a member.

A tremendous force existing in almost every pastorate is the pressure of the denominational image. If the former pastor was what is called "a denominational man," then the new pastor is in for trouble. He does not want to be labeled as a nonconformist nor as uncooperative, so he gives his time grudgingly to meetings and sessions he cannot honestly appreciate. His church gives to the unified budget of his denomination and he feels that to represent his people he must cooperate to some degree. He knows that unless he becomes a rubber stamp to some extent that he will not be appointed to boards. If this happens, he will be letting his church down, so his people think. His predecessor was one of the "boys" of the denomination and thereby heaped many honors on his church by being appointed to the various boards, etc. Now the present pastor has to fill these shoes and the *pressure of the denominational system is powerful.* It takes a strong man to withstand this pressure of the existing images, and so it is rare that a pastor goes to a new church unfettered. He is in chains before he moves into the parsonage.

While the image of a parson is freighted with the lack of definitiveness and bogged down with cultural patterns, there is the ever-present ray of light in this darkness. In each congregation there is that group of people who have such a pure love of God and who are so involved in spirit that their conception of the pastoral office is most healthy. They see him as a brother and fellow journeyman who is himself trying to experience the Kingdom of God and who is trying to help others to do the same. The difference is that he is trained academically to guide their thought patterns to more wholesome conclusions. They want him to study much and to prepare diligently for the sermons he brings to them and they do not desire that he become a gad-about-town. In fact they would be disappointed if he were that type of person.

These people do not demand that he be aware of their every ache and pain and they look out for him and his family, knowing the impossible task he has of trying to minister to many people. They want him to be free to speak clearly on the issues and would be the last to force him into a mold. There is a small but wonderfully refreshing generation of young churchmen who are appearing on the scene. They are a good complement to the many genuinely sincere people in the churches because they also see the pastor as a man of integrity and honor. Their image of him is as one of the under-shepherds of Christ's flock, and as such he is dear to their hearts. Their respect for this office abides even when some fail to measure up to its high standards. Their view is one of the office and then of the different men as they come and go. This office and the man who occupies it are not available as subjects of street talk gossip. These devout people would be the last to criticize their pastor. There are these people in every congregation and it is a sure thing that these are the wonderful folks who are responsible for what little solidarity there is left to the pastoral ranks. They give strength and meaning to a man when he is constantly besieged by the menacing images his culture thrusts upon him.

3

The Cult Development

*Some people are so busy learning the tricks of the trade
that they never learn the trade.*—VERN LAW

The term "cult" is offensive to most people. It smacks of
ignorance, superstition and deceit. A cult is characterized
by its attendant symbols, hidden meanings, dress, mannerisms, speech and world view, as well as other indications
of a particular mind-set. With such a definition it must be
categorically stated that the pastoral ministry in large segment is a cult. This also cuts across denominational lines
and includes men in teaching positions and denominational posts. It is as one layman said, "I can spot a preacher
a block away." This is not idle talk. If one knows what to
look for, he can notice a minister in any crowd and this
without the formal clerical collar.

This man of the cult has learned the language and knows

when to use it. He has been able to dress appropriately and to use articulate phrases with a particular *tonal* quality. Somehow, when this disease gets to a man, it is hard for him to get free from it. Some men have conscientiously tried to free themselves from this stigma, but find it much more difficult than they thought it would be. There is a certain security within the cult. Before a lengthy discussion is needed on cultist tendencies, it would be worth our while to attempt to find a reason for the formation of the cult development.

As was stated in chapter One, the pastoral ministry suffers from a lack of definition all the way back to its birth. This lack of some definite structural lines has opened the door for interpretations from every quarter as to the meaning of the office. It is only natural that the pastors themselves would attempt at a crystallizing of their role. They would, like any other group, attempt to give a picture of what a pastor is like and this honest effort toward the development of the picture of the man and his office has opened the door wider for all kinds of weird and wild patterns of behavior. By and large, a few clear lines of behavioral patterns are seen. These involve the man and his office, and shockingly enough, sometimes these amount to a development of just another cult in which the clergy has become a kind of separate branch of the church. This is a purposeful development in the Roman Church and while many Protestant bodies vigorously denounce the idea that the clergy is a separate group, they must admit that the Protestant clergy on the whole is a class in itself and has every distinguishable characteristic of the cult development.

Protestantism takes pride in the fact that its ministers are a part of the people and not separated by class distinction. *This is just not true!* For the most part, it is just the opposite. This is not to say that there is *one* and only one designation of the Protestant ministry, because there are groups within the total grouping. Sadly enough there is very *little* individuality within the ranks of ministers and when a real individualist comes along, he is noticed immediately and usually provides a distinct contribution to the pastoral office and image. At this stage, it is sufficient to say that there are many more conformists to the cult than nonconformists. Sometimes even the nonconformists fall into patterns of group behavior. Rarely does a true individualist come along who defies conformity to any one set mold.

There is a basic need in all human beings for identification with some group. This need for identity involves a sense of seeking after security. Certainly with the absence of rigid and detailed guidelines for the life and work of the pastor and with his office thrown into a world of changing standards and cultural patterns, there arose the legitimate need of some definite lines for identification purposes. A person could point to these characteristics and try to obtain those he did not have. Eventually, the young pastor becomes initiated into the cult. This becomes no more or less than playing the role. Whether this is good or bad is a value judgment left to the reader. The truth of the matter is that many pastors play a role from morning till dark. Their families see them in an altogether different light than the one in which they are seen by the church members.

The one great area of decimated returns on his investment of time and energy could well be from his own family. Wives and children must secretly resent this role-playing. There are, however, some women who are heard to address their husbands by the title of "Reverend" or "brother" instead of his first name like most other men's wives. This they do when referring to him before the other members of the congregation. This type of wife has joined her husband in role playing. Children of pastors are acutely aware of their father's role and the pastor should make every point of being himself before his children. Of course, this is what he should be all the time, but not so for those cultists who prefer role-playing, and their masks are secure.

The development of a young novice for receiving his credentials for cult membership begins quite early. Many of the young candidates for the ministry decide during high school or the early days in college and these are tender years and most formative for the young man. His first few years are as formative for his ministry as were the first few years after his birth for his development as a human being. He gets to preach a few times and this greatly kindles the fire. First sermons are at times pathetically humorous. A doctor is not permitted to perform surgery by himself until sufficient training has been given for his "solo" performance. The young aspirant to the ministry is not spared from his fright, but usually his first congregation is loving and considerate of his first attempt at a safe landing. Sometimes the lad cannot get off the ground, then sometimes those who do sail on and on and on. They are so taken with their new wings that they never want to come down and sometimes they don't, either for that hour and for the rest of their ministry. It is not fair to the gospel to start a young man in a preaching career too early. This work is far too serious to have it in the hands of novices.

The young preacher immediately looks about him for older men as his pattern and this is only natural. Some are rather conservative, or it should be said that most young men are conservative. Strangely enough, most younger men try to copy what will be called for lack of a better term a cultist. They by now have already learned to suspect the individualist. He presents something of an enigma to them. The older pastor who is playing the cultist role is easy to mimic, so he becomes the pattern for the younger man. These young men are often sadly let down when their older, more successful examples are seen to have feet of clay.

The problem of the continuance of the cult can be traced to this source. Individualists are difficult to put into categories of behavioral patterns, and because of the human tendency toward emulation, the majority is copied in every detail and the cult continues. The first glance at this phenomenon in Biblical history is seen in the sparse accounts of the bands of prophets in the days of Elisha when these schools of the prophets were many. They were of Israel but the great and contradictory truth is that the prophets who are canonized in thought and description were rugged individualists and did not belong to these schools. One would think that the new Israel would learn from the old Israel but lessons from history are seldom heeded until it is too late.

For a description of the basic patterns of the cult and the emulation of the younger men, a good start would be his mannerisms. Before any real attempt is made at his way of life, the reader will immediately recall the earlier chapter on the images of him that are in the layman's mind. A legitimate question involves the truth of the layman's conceptions of the pastoral ministry. If a cult is described, isn't the layman right in assuming some of the images mentioned in chapter Two? The answer is "yes." The question, however, is one of the chicken and the egg—which came first? Did the layman's pressures, which are seen in Paul's letters, force the development of the cult for the safety of the pastors or did the pastors develop their cult first and as a result the layman's images arise from observation and experiences with these men? The answer is not important for this study. More than likely there is truth in both views. What is true is that *there are conceptional images* the layman has and enforces on his pastor and *there is a cult* that has all the attendant symbols and meanings that many pastors subscribe to.

When one writer of the New Testament desired that God's people be a "peculiar race" he evidently was taken to mean that they were to be odd! That we preachers are an odd group is not debatable in most quarters but what makes us odd is hard to determine. It is a sure thing that one or a number of us can be spotted in a crowd. Some have thought that the answer is one of purpose, that the cultist wants to be considered a "man of God." He wants to stand out from the average man and as such he gets his wish.

Nowhere is the emulation of mannerisms more noticeable than in the pulpit. The young seminary student goes back to his preaching post and tries to preach like the chapel speaker from River City. He holds his hands a certain way and gestures the same way his hero does and even his Scripture reading has the same quality with voice inflection rising and falling the way he has observed. The young cultist learns to gather extremely sad stories because he has observed their power in the persuasion of people. He knows exactly where to put these stories into his sermon's framework and this leads to a delivery that is easily recognizable as not being his but someone else's. Soon it becomes *his* style and he is on his way to becoming a full-fledged member of the cult.

An evangelist who became prominent some years ago used a rapid style of delivery when he was on the radio, and it caused many young preachers to preach fast. They thought that the preacher's power was in his delivery. What they didn't know was that he was reading from a manuscript carefully prepared for this type of rapid fire presentation for effect and conservation of time.

Any discussion of the cultist's preaching sooner or later has to mention his tonal quality. This type of minister soon learns a way of talking that is peculiar to the cult of preachers and is a language all to itself. There is a certain nasal quality to the pitch of the voice. There is a way to pronounce the word "God" that is one clear trademark of the cult. When one of these men walks into the presence of a group of men, the first sentence he states is "preachery" and most noticeable. The young pastor soon learns this "language of Zion" as it has been called facetiously. *Why an average cultist can't talk like a normal individual is beyond the comprehension of most clear-thinking folks.* This way of talking is most offensive when it is employed in a sing-song effect in the pulpit. This is accompanied by a redness of the neck and a near loss of breath as the preacher thunders away and his preaching is punctuated by gasps for breath. In between his thoughts he injects the name of the Lord Jesus Christ over and over again or he supplies a deluge of platitudes and meaningless phrases. These are only used to fill up space and help him to find his place, which he lost in the heat of action.

Invariably, the cultist will describe this way of preaching and delivery as "spirit-led." The extremes to which a man will go to attract attention to his point are ridiculous. Some have jumped up on the pulpit stand or on a piano, or have broken chairs, and these spells are all considered to be dynamically induced by the power of God. These cultist marks are less distinguishable as one observes the more orthodox pastor of the Presbyterian Church, for instance, over against that of one of the Pentecostal sects. Still, they have the same characteristics of the cult in many instances. Some are just a little more polished than others.

These stained-glass, holy-toned cultists are a real hindrance to the work of sincere pastors. Not that some of these "holy Joe" type pastors are not sincere, but one wonders why they continue to talk this way when certainly their manner of speaking is so unrealistic. The young aspirant to the ministry would do well to watch carefully his speech patterns because this type of sermon is almost like a disease that is hard to get rid of. If the young pastor would just talk normally, he might free himself from the other cultist characteristics as well.

In the past a cultist characteristic was one of dress. This is not as apparent as it once was because men's styles in clothing have improved. Many Protestant ministers have for a long time made remarks about the clerical collars worn by some men as a designated uniform. In reality most of those who made derogatory remarks about this practice were dressed in black except for the white shirt. They wore the same style of shoe, of a French-toe design that shoe clerks actually called in some stores their "preacher shoes." The younger men tried to dress older than their years. One of the brightest hopes that is visualized in the cult is this one of dress. Even though most of the men hold rigidly to the jargon and to a mushmouth way of talking, their dress is becoming more contemporary. It is hoped that from the change in the outward appearance there can be seen an ideological change in the thinking of the young cultist. He will change, when he gets sick enough of himself.

Another distinguishable characteristic of the typical cultist is that of his view of the Bible's inspiration. He will be a literalist for the most part, making the Bible a textbook on history, science, astronomy and religion. He will constantly thunder phrases in which he says he believes the Bible from cover to cover. He never fully describes what he believes it to say because he is so busy saying that he believes it. It is all on the same level of inspiration to him. Some men have been known to prove segregation by the Bible, just as their forefathers proved slavery by the very same Book. They have been known to lead in Bible burnings of versions that were "liberal," such as the *Revised Standard Version.* Incidentally, the term "liberal" is the dirtiest word they know, unless it is the word "modernist." The cultist is never more in character than when he is seen in hot pursuit of the liberals within the ranks of his own denomination or wherever he can find them. The cult has its own special breed of hounds.

Aside from the cultist's ultraconservative doctrinal

positions and his incessant attacks on what he calls liberalism, there is his code of social ethics. At this point, it is to be made perfectly clear that the convictions a man has concerning dancing, drinking, playing cards, and a host of other activities are certainly not being made light of. What is resented is the typical cultist attitude represented by the question, "Should a preacher or his family be *seen* doing these things?" It is not that he has a conviction about the evil involved, it is his *role* that he is most concerned with. This hypocrisy is seen when the pastor will smoke away from his church people and attend movies with his family in another town. No greater hypocrisy is to be found than for that man to preach about integrity on Sunday. Moralistic legalism is the main theme of the ministry of many of these men.

The cult is continually considering its conduct not so much for real conviction's sake as for the continuance of the image of something they are not! This leads to a type of hypocrisy and bigotry unbecoming to Christ's servants. The sincere pastor is always given heed by his flock but if he is playing a role his people soon catch on. They will do one of two things.

The first thing that some laymen will do is to join the cult from a sort of lay-membership vantage point. These people will begin to play the role with the pastor and a little group of self-righteous folks will be formed with the congregation. Strangely enough some of the "cultist laymen" can outdo their pastors. They have learned well! They can pray with the same wordy and stained-glass tones. They like to identify readily with pastors and other ministers and have become contentious in some sections of the country where they are known as lay-preachers. There is nothing wrong with lay-preachers as such but the cultist breed is more rigidly narrow and vicious than its pastor teachers could ever be. They make the best Pharisees of all!

One typical pastor of this vintage founded a lay-preacher group that met to pray on Saturday nights and became a real power structure within the church; in fact, it was almost a church within the church. The group was legalistic, and each man carried a Bible wherever he went because it was a symbol to him. To the horror of the pastor several of them walked into his office one Sunday and told him that he had been at the church long enough. They said he had lost his "power" and that *they* could preach as well as he. This is nothing more than zeal run wild and when the cult has given birth to these self-righteous creatures nothing but havoc reigns in the church community.

The second thing that happens when a cultist successfully gets his ideas across is that those who won't play the role with him will slowly fade away from church or try to join a church in which integrity is more important than what they have witnessed. Sometimes these conscientious people will patiently wait until a new pastor can come and then pray that he will not be a cultist. Now the people don't know how to articulate the ideas represented here in a description of the cult development but what is more important, *they know one when they see one* because a great percentage of men are like this.

One of the distinguishing marks of a cultist is the picture of the pastor on the go. Nothing so characterizes a pastor like going, for he is constantly on the go. This pressure on him to be on the go has caused a most unusual reaction. The typical cult pastor *really likes* the business of going. Now he will tell his congregation that he is so busy going to important functions that he wishes he had time to stop and study or be with his family. This is simply not so! There is a certain amount of the forsaking of responsibility in being in a car between meetings. Pastors go because they want to go!

Methodist Bishop Gerald H. Kennedy wrote this same sentiment concerning his denomination. The *Christian Advocate* quotes him as saying, "Most of the business at the meetings could be accomplished by letter or telephone. . . . And maybe in place of those endless, circling, repetitious gatherings we might begin to be a people who read their Bibles and gather silently to hear His voice." He suggested a four-year period of elimination of those meetings, which cost his denomination $2,225,000 a year in travel alone.

It needs to be stated succinctly and the whistle blown for all to hear. The endless number of denominational meetings are designed to do two things mainly. One is to justify the position of the denominational officer whose meeting or program it is and the other is to give the undisciplined pastor another place to go. Pastors are notoriously bad about keeping office hours. Their pretense is that they are in church-planning sessions but in reality they are going to or coming from some *senseless meeting*.

An intelligent layman would be appalled at the lack of planning and lack of genuine depth of the average denominational meeting, at which the cult pastors take turns preaching or teaching or promoting some phase of the church's work. The meetings of this sort are subterfuge to give some lazy pastors a place to go. They get up at these meetings and laugh about their lack of preparation for their time on the program or if they do give a prepared part, it is the same six and seven. If a man does any serious thinking in most denominational meetings it would be such a shock some would never get over it. Many denominational meetings are puppet shows at which participants declare that their denomination is the best with the most and intone the statistics to prove it. It is reasonably doubted whether statistics prove or disprove anything in church work. Constantine baptized his entire army with wet tree branches. He could have had a good showing in the yearly church statistical columns and been elected president of his convention.

The picture of the man on the go is painted by some pastors for a purpose and it is a deceptive one. It is to fool the people, to serve as a means for impressing them with his "much work." It is a guise to waste time! When a disciplined pastor follows one of this breed it is hard on him until he breaks the cultist's strangle hold on the people. One such pastor tells of his first church out of the seminary where it seems that he tried to set up office hours, but his people violently objected. He tried to study hard and long but they accused him of not doing anything but hiding away in his office, and they talked of the former pastor and how he worked so hard. (That he had worked hard was evidenced by his much going.) The people reminded him that their last pastor was always "on the go." He assured them jokingly that they could not adequately judge a man's ministry by his wearing out tire tread.

One Monday morning, he told his wife he could not be reached by phone until noon and that this pattern would keep up all week. He used two tanks of gasoline and just rode constantly up and down the road and streets. He drank enough coffee to ruin his kidneys and he spoke to everyone he could see. This pace continued all week, and sure enough, he was exhausted by Saturday. When he arrived at the church for Sunday school, a deacon motioned for him to come over to a group of men who were talking. When he got to the group he was pleasantly surprised to hear them say that it was the talk of the town that he was really out among the people all the past week. He had been good companionship for practically everyone's coffee break. They assured him that he would have a good pastorate if he kept that up.

Honest he was, and so he wiped the smile from his face and told the men what he had done, that he had not said a word for Christ, that he had talked of nothing but hunting and fishing and that he had not meditated, prayed or studied. He had simply wanted to show them that they could not judge by a man's much going whether he is working at being a good pastor or not. They got the point and appreciated his real ministry from that day on.

Then some of this cult variety go all the time because they really don't apply themselves to their church work. Now one of the images the layman has is that of the pastor who doesn't do anything. The layman is *so right* about the typical cultist and he has nailed him to the wall. The typical cultist is guilty of the worst of sins for a pastor and that sin is laziness. When a man works at his job, no matter what size the church is he is never through. On the other hand, it is typical of many pastors not to have office hours because they do not want to have the responsibility of being there. Any discipline is too much for them. They are enamored with the here, there and everywhere routine.

The pastor for the most part is self-employed and yet he is on salary and this means that he draws the same salary whether he is busy or not. The cult pastor is laziest at the point of study and sermon preparation. There has been a deluge of the most pitiful preaching in the recent history of the church and it is a result of two contributing factors. The first is the number of times a man has to preach, which has already been stated. Two or three times a week are too many for adequate preparation. It has already been posited that this frustration breeds a second rate effort on Sundays, especially Sunday nights. This half-hearted approach finally wears off on all the pastor's work and he becomes a typical cultist throwing out three-point hash sprinkled with pious platitudes. It is more an extemporaneous showmanship than Biblical preaching.

The second contributing factor to the cultist's poor preaching is that he is not an integrated personality. Many pastors are dominated by their wives. They have to pick up the children at school, go grocery shopping or baby-sit at all hours of the day when they should be studying. The discipline of hard study is too much for many pastors.

This is a place where the slothful man can be lazy; this work can be the easiest in all society or it can be the hardest, and it takes a real dedicated and committed Christian pastor to keep from succumbing to the temptation of idleness. Poor preaching arises from poor preparation and there is nothing quite as hard as preparing a sermon. On the other hand, there is nothing quite as easy as grabbing at three shallow and pithy ideas. The man who is lazy at study has the time to be all over the community and this makes it hard on the real student when it is expected that he do the same.

Pastors have time to spend on petty things or in real work, and study is hard work if it is regular. One divinity school graduate aptly stated his case when he held up his diploma saying, "This is my union card. I can go most anywhere with this degree, no more hitting the books for me." Laziness has many avenues and the pastor is in a position to create a façade because no one can really tell whether he is busy or not. The pastor is blessed with the privilege of being the sole organizer of his time, if he has the desire to guide his people.

There are many guises of laziness. Some men refuse to tackle situations under the guise of "maturity and patience" when the truth is that they are fearful of the work entailed in facing the problem. This is the type of laziness referred here. There are a lot of ways to be slothful other than physically.

The spineless kind of man who makes up the cult is never a voice; he is only an echo of his culture. Yes, he booms out about vice running rampant in the nation's capital and he lashes out at drunkards and the liquor industry but he never seems to say anything that indicates he has any prophetic ministry whatsoever.

One of the most humorous episodes in this vein was witnessed several years ago in Kentucky. It seems that a young preacher in one of the seminaries in Louisville had a weekend preaching post. He was known for his violent stand on the use of alcohol. Like most seminary students, he did not have an overabundance of money and this little church offered him enough financial security to go through school. The first Sunday he was there he barely got to the church in time to preach. He noticed the big barn-like houses all around the church property and dotting the hillside behind the church. His church school superintendent had a pin on his lapel indicating twenty-five years employment in none other than a distillery. The prime source of income in that church was from employment in the distillery. It is safe to say that he never preached a sermon on the evil of the liquor business while he was there.

The story actually happened and the point is to be well taken. In the great struggles of our time the typical cultist is caught in the anachronism of seeing "how the wind blows" before he commits himself. These men never know if they are attracted to a thing or repulsed by it. Whatever a man preaches against the most is likely to be the thing *he* is most attracted to. Most men are uncertain of everything but the desire for their own security. For example, some of the cult in low income congregations are heard to criticize people with money, mainly for that fact alone. They sing songs and preach wordy sermons about heaven with its golden streets and a big mansion for everyone. The cult development is never seen in a more sordid picture than when the pastor is just a voice telling the people what they already believe and what they want to hear.

This very shallow approach to the Christian ministry is also seen in the cult of numbers. This should be called the *preacher's numbers game* and it is about as far from the New Testament as the numbers game is illegal. In this environment the cult pastor builds each service around the figures he can count and sometimes juggle to impress people. This has centered mainly in the Sunday school where some men have been known to count people who come early for worship and add them to the Sunday school

attendance. Some have been known to simply overesti-
mate purposely in case "they missed someone." Some
churches even run attendance races with other churches of
equal size. This has to be called a children's game. There
is one *real reason* for this numbers fad. It is for the con-
struction of a *grand and glorious image of the pastor* and
he will use this as a means of promoting his own craving
for recognition.

Many churches must de-emphasize their big business
attitude and their Madison Avenue promotional characteristics. People have had their fill of lengthy promotional
announcements on Sunday morning when the bulletin is
read through for people who also can read. What a waste
of time! *The man in the pew has been promoted to death
by the man in the bowl.* People have long enough been
manipulated solely for the sake of larger budgets and more
and impressively larger buildings, which only inflate the
ego of the pastor and people. The service must be a place
of worship where man meets God, not where men try to
outdo each other. People have had enough harassment
sugar-coated with a religious whip that marshals them into
line. The pastor manipulating people for the aggrandizement of his own ego and wish for fulfillment has forced
many good and sincere people away from the eleven
o'clock service and away from church.

Eleven o'clock, or whenever the time of corporate worship is stated, is not the time for gimmicks and campaigns
for attendance in the church school. These cheap attend-

ance campaigns typified by the silliest of all, "Be one of the Bunch," displaying a string of paper bananas each bearing a person's name, has sounded taps for the church unless its mentality rises above this level. Could it possibly be that the pastors who promote attendance with such senseless means have that level of mentality? May God help the recruit if the general is drunk on that wine!

A cultist like this seeks to manipulate people because it gives him a sense of power to have people in his hands so he can marshal them here and there. The endless promotion of numbers will get some men by with their congregations. As one man said, "I can't preach so I have to promote the program!" So often the shallow-minded layman feeds on this endless diet of meetings at the church. Each meeting is to promote another meeting and sometimes it is difficult to determine whether the meeting is to realize an *end* or promote a *means*. In other words they are not sure if they are "doing or getting prepared to do."

The cultist is forever maneuvering his image before his people. He impresses them with how much he does by dropping the names of several people that he just happened to see and for whom he wants them to pray. He has the philosophy that if he doesn't blow his own horn it will not be blown and he must manipulate people for his own ends. He can't preach without forcing some kind of reaction at the close of the service. This extended invitation and emotional appeal is to gratify his own banal response to his preaching. He is told to preach for decisions and does this quite adequately. However, each of us should seriously search our motives. The cultist finds satisfaction in mass hypnosis effects on his congregation and is never happier than when they are "walking the aisle."

That there is truth to the idea of mass hypnotic effects on a congregation is not challenged seriously anywhere from people who have some grasp of group behavior under certain conditions. An example of this occurs in some faith healing groups in which the cult preacher will take an offering three or four times during the service. The time *has to be right* and he is dedicated to the observance of those moments of hypnotic spells.

Congregational manipulation is best seen in some of the professional evangelists who are no more than recruiters. That the New Testament word for *evangelist* is equivalent to our modern day *missionaries* is not a deterrent at all to this phenomenon. There is little parallel in the New Testament to some of the gaudy side-show type revival meetings in many sections of the country today. Certainly super-pious answers sugar-coated with New Testament phraseology and those without proper textual exegesis are not wanted by this forthcoming generation of seeking laymen. Doing the work of an evangelist is the duty of every Christian.

Some professional evangelists on the other hand, are marked by several distinguishing characteristics, not all of which could be called "Christian." First, it must be said that they are cultists, and have all the tones of voice, all the symbolic phrases that dedicate them publicly to a steadfast belief in the Bible, the virgin birth and three or four other statements of orthodoxy. They must vehemently blast modernists, liberals, cold-hearted Christians and vices of all kinds, the worst of which is strong drink. They have a role they play to the hilt. This role includes their dress. Amazingly enough when the cultist pastor is busy trying to dress "like a pastor should" the cultist evangelist is allowed the privilege of "dressing like an evangelist should." This includes the gaudiest of clothes; and the first impression of some evangelists is of a real Hollywood type of atmosphere. His sport coats are as loud as his voice and his Bible (always *King James Version*) has a red back. Some even have a different colored Bible for each occasion and suit color. This could be called Bible "tones." It is not unusual to hear the average citizen talking about the many-colored suits of these evangelists. In fact, this has become a greater selling feature for attendance than their preaching. They will give a sad story generally about the need for money and the gullible layman will put more money into the coffer.

Another characteristic of the huckster of religion is his long hair. Long before the present rage for long hair, some professional evangelists cultivated a mane of wavy hair, through which they could run their hands while preaching. Usually, they have a hair stylist to give the right slant of profile for pictures for advance publicity. Typical publicity always includes the promise that the greatest of God's servants has yet to come to town. It amounts to the same thing philosophically as the show business theme of "You Ain't Heard Nothing Yet!" One picture of our hero will always show him holding a Bible high or clutched to his heart. Then with a finger pointed toward heaven or straight ahead he gives the impression of real action. This pose would have to have its counterpart in the ads that describe action-packed adventure in movies. This type of evangelist promises the crowds something they have never seen before. They have, however, but it was called legitimate vaudeville!

The fact of the matter is that there is nothing new to these men. Most churches of their persuasion have these side show antics once or twice a year; the stark tragedy is that a generation of church people have been born and raised on this and look forward to it once or twice a year. It has become a narcotic to them and they get their shots in the spring and late summer. Some people don't attend church very often between the big shows. Sometimes these events are held in tents, which gives the impression of the "big top" event. Even the cultist pastor falls for the routine that real religion is outside the walls of his expensive church plant, so he arranges a tent on a parking lot or sometimes on the church property itself and brings in the showman.

The cultist evangelist is in reality cutting the heart out of the pastor, but the latter is so exceedingly stupid he can't see the light. Our evangelist thunders away and thrills with his stories of scenes out of the Book (sometimes out of reality), while the pastor sits either on the platform or on the front row and nods or amens affirmatively. His people follow in the incantation of the moment and before the poor pastor realizes it the people are saying to themselves, "Our pastor is so dry and dull, wouldn't it be wonderful to have this fellow for a pastor? Just think of the thrill of having this show twice on Sunday instead of twice a year." Many pastors have had to leave churches after these meetings because plain vanilla is tasteless after a banana split.

Now, the cult evangelist as a pastor is a good thought. Just where did these creatures come from? It may shock the average layman to know that most of them are former *cultist pastors.* They had trouble in their own churches so they have set out on the road of the itinerant evangelist; besides, the pay is much better.

One pastor tells of an experience in college in which a young ministerial student failed his courses. He was a bright young man with a flare for the dramatic. When it was apparent that he had to leave school, he exclaimed to his friends, "I am going into professional evangelism. I can make three times as much as these professors in my first year." The next thing anyone knew about him was an ad they saw with his picture against the skyline of a big city with an "evangelistic association" behind his work. At last account he owned an interest in land development and was making money at a rate the average reader would not believe. These men draw several hundred dollars a week and some, the bigger names, as much as a thousand dollars. A quick count would reveal that an Internal Revenue Service check of this group would be a full-time job. Some have radio programs and literature they mail out.

Some of the men offer added services, such as faith-healing techniques. An added feature to some meetings is the plea for money by our evangelist because he is away from his wife and children. So are salesmen for drug companies, insurance firms and other sales service organizations. The gospel "wholesaler" must take that into consideration. Anyway, he should not make so much more money than the "retailer" he calls on. His job is made easier by the small number of sermons he has to preach. He can polish them to a brilliant luster and memorize all the Scripture. His crowd (not congregation) will go away rejoicing in his ability to *quote the good Book* and to *preach without notes* because these two virtues are sure signs of the call of God on a man. The poor pastor can't follow this routine of grandeur but is it his fault for inviting this fellow in the first place, or did his laymen demand it?

Now just why are these men around and why does a pastor have them? One answer is found in the advertising of the fellow. He is successful at reaping a harvest of souls. He can really bring in the sheaves. He advertises himself by his previous campaigns in local churches or in football stadiums. *He can produce.* Many have suggested that while reaping is one phase of the New Testament approach to evangelism, there is another, and that is sowing the seed.

It is wondered how many revivals these recruiters would get if they advertised themselves as sowers and their previous work was sowing to large crowds. The answer is obvious, they would be as extinct as the dinosaur overnight. That is why the cult evangelist is around. He is here to aid the cult pastor in acquiring new converts. The denominational pressure exerted on a pastor to show numerical gains in membership has given rise to this creature. He will manipulate the younger folks into a type of group reaction hysteria and baptize all those old enough to get exposed. *The harm this type of thing has done to the church is beyond words.* A part of our predicament can be laid at the feet of the cultist pastor, and his twice-a-year recruiter, whipping up a lather of frenzy that is better known for its high percentage of "fallout."

Someone will always come back with the answer of his conversion and that it was genuine. The end has never justified the means in Christianity. David Brainard was said to have preached to some Indians on one occasion while using a drunk Indian as an interpreter. That some people are converted doesn't mean that the truly unhealthy atmosphere of these revival displays is justified. Some laymen are so carried away that they send money periodically to these men. How gullible can some people be?

The cult pastor will dislike many of the tricks of the trade of these fellows such as having personal workers designated to come forward at the start of the invitation to get things moving. However, the pastor continues to support them. One of the characteristics of these men is that they must have a lurid background of violence—almost gangsterism—before they "saw the light." This story of their own conversion is told with a big buildup and this usually comes toward the end of the week after the first hypnotic spell is wearing off. This autobiographical sketch grows each time it is told and is very, very exciting to hear; in fact, it is fast becoming the one big night. This usually causes Mr. or Mrs. Average Church Member to doubt his own personal salvation because he didn't have that kind of experience. In these meetings an effort is obviously made to show that there is *nothing normal* about anything. One cannot have a good saving experience unless he has really become "dirty in sin." Sin is sometimes described in retrospect by these drummers so that some of the young people get their appetites whetted. He tells about having had a mistress, then after this is explained in detail, he tells how bad it was. It did not sound bad, as he told it!

Another reason the pastors keep sponsoring these men is that they go from church to church and are in contact with laymen. The cult pastor is always looking for a recommendation from the cult evangelist, so it is a type of reciprocal arrangement between them, a type of "you scratch my back, and I will scratch yours!" It is wondered if there is room for *any* of them or not. The layman who reads these words must say to his pastor that he is tired of being used and manipulated. These abuses of the dignity of the office will be stopped most quickly when the layman quits *footing the bill.* Stop the flow of money as these men have been used to it and they will cease to be "effective." *Laymen should not attend these circus-like meetings.*

When the cult evangelists put on their acts most people are so entertained that they say, "Church was never like this before!" Let us hope not. So much for the cult evangelist. *May he become extinct!*

No discussion of the cultist development in the pastoral ranks would be complete without a discussion of cult pastor's desire for denominational standing. He is ever playing politics. He courts the favor of his bishop or his ranking denominational officer. He will use his church to preach every program his denominational leaders offer. This is easier than thinking on his own. He constantly wants an increase in money for the denominational needs. This he piously calls missions and beats his people into subjection by implications of "God's leadership." This psychological whip can get the job done most of the time. His denominational officers are proud of him and the ever-increasing revenue into the district or state office. They will see to it that he is branded "cooperative," "up and coming," "on fire" and "just the man for that larger church"! The cult pastor has wedded himself to the denomination. The only thing lost in this marriage is *sight.*

Also, he ever aspires for denominational posts and titles. To be president of the district or state group would be a "foretaste of glory divine." This brings up the subject of

the cult pastor's desire for a larger flock. He is never satisfied where he is and he is ever looking for another congregation. He uses his people as steppingstones to achieve
the heights of fame and fortune he is seeking. He counts
pulpit committees and places his name before them in
ingenious ways and he even uses them as guests to get a
raise in salary from his own people who hoping their "pastor will not leave us."

Many denominational meetings are run from beginning
to end by the cultists. In fact, to coin a phrase, the "cultists
of the cult" are in control much of the time. This meeting
is a thing of wonder, truly a "bird of paradise." As one
layman who went for the first time declared, "I never saw
anything like it or got so little out of so much. I hope I
never have to go to another one." It is characterized by a
flood of reassurances that there is really nothing wrong
with the church and statistics are juggled for obvious reasons. Each denominational department gets to have its
time to gloat over the progress of the past year. Most
pastors stay in the lobby during these reports yet maintain
their necessity. Such *clear thinking* is further characterized at these meetings with a barrage of preaching about
the cold-hearted folks who make up churches. Of course,
those "cold-hearted" folks are paying the convention ex-
pense of these fellows.

Perhaps the best description of these meetings is the
complete absence of provocative addresses. All sermons
must be noncontroversial and sugar-coated with cultic

ideas to the core. Any controversy must come during the special times called for during the miscellaneous business sessions. There is much heat generated at these meetings but very little light.

Another characteristic is that the "greats" pass across the stage. These are those pastors who have been superb cultists and have "gone far." Seldom does a rugged individualist get a spot on the program, but even the cult evangelist, if he is one of the "name stars," gets a billing. He preaches at one of the more rousing sessions and it is said that most of these delegates get as many as ten sermon outlines at these most "meaningful" meetings.

Many denominational meetings are an inspiration for the further development of the cult because we seldom have the courage to openly criticize our work and we labor under a facade of dishonesty.

So far the ideas have revolved around the conformist cultist pastor. Some mention must be made of a type of nonconformist. He is rapidly forming a cult development all his own. He is characterized by his desire to be different from the descriptions previously mentioned. He wants to be characterized as intelligent, sophisticated and contemporary and he too is all things to all men in the wrong ways. There is a growing group of these people who use dirty language purposely in an effort to be accepted. They condemn the institutional church without regard or love for its welfare and they are only one step away from the beatnik philosophy. Some of these men read filthy literature under the guise of the need to learn "what is going on," so they say.

One characteristic of these nonconformists is that they do not use the Bible much, if any. How they were ordained is a good question. These men are ever seen as a breed of new Gnostics always posing and never getting or wanting answers. They are rapidly becoming *the cult of the coffee house* and will undercut the real needs of the church as much as the other extreme in question in this chapter. As yet this breed is so new that a detailed study of their development would be premature.

Why are men in this tradition of cult characteristics? Why, in the face of facts that may not have found their way into print but are *well known* to the average pastor? These things are discussed at length in one way or another by pastors when they get together. The answer to the continuation and further development of *any cult is one of security.* The cult pastor is the most insecure man in the community. There is insecurity because of the many reasons previously mentioned concerning the predicament of the man. The cult development is none other than a *massive defense mechanism for his own security.* He is like a man without bearings. While on the one hand he steadfastly declares his faith in God in sermon, on the other hand he is afraid of his own shadow.

The cult pastor runs scared. He is frightened of his members, of their attitude toward him, of their demands on his life, of their criticism and even of their complimentary remarks. He is frightened of the latter because he doesn't know how to interpret them or just why the person said what he did. The cultist is truly a frightened man and he will resort to anything for peace of mind—short, that is, of being a truly independent individual. This takes courage, the one characteristic so noticeably missing in many pastors today.

The continuation of the development of the cult will not soon spend its force. There is no foreseeable end to it. It has been with us since New Testament times and was seen earlier in the prophets' schools. It is the one great paradox of the Christian ministry for it is the cultist pastor's strength and *security* while at the same time it is his *downfall.* It gives him enough machinery to go on but it cripples him to the extent that he can never be the *individual* God meant him to be.

4

The Audience Mentality

The church through her worship... helps us to live with lasting things.—RALPH W. SOCKMAN

In Biblical days, the people were gathered to experience the presence of God and there was no theatrical characteristic in any degree. Any attempt to refer to the priestly functions as a bit of theatrics is without sufficient knowledge of the moral overtones of these priestly acts. The congregation was involved in the hush of realizing the presence of God. The solemnness of the priestly ritual stands out most vividly to the student of the life of Israel.

Somewhere along the way we lost this sense of coming together to experience the Presence and much of Christianity has become an hour of religious entertainment that has led to what I would call the audience mentality. It has not spent its force to this day and perhaps sadly enough as long as the institutional church "performs" its Sunday ritual the audience mentality will be with us.

The letters of the New Testament are filled with references to Paul's attempts to regulate the attitude and actions of "the people set free from the laws of Judaism." For instance, some of them frustrated the meaning of the Last Supper memorial when they were enjoying a feast instead of a symbolic memorial to a greater meaning. There was also a dastardly comparison of "preachers and their sway over the people." Paul himself was accused of being strong with the pen, but he did not cut too classic a picture of persuasive preaching when he was face to face with the people. In fact, they indicated that he could barely hold their attention—shades of later years. The poor fellow was not imposing in his pulpit appearance and was certainly not the dashing speaker this young church at Corinth needed. What happened we shall never know, but somewhere between the freedom that the new covenant brought and the repudiation of the old system of blood sacrifice and priestly ritual, the Church of Jesus Christ lost some real guidelines for public worship.

Few scholars will indicate in any way that they believe Jesus envisioned an institutional church as we know it today but He came to bring the cup to overflowing, not to crack it to pieces, which may be what many of us have done. He was not pleased with the pitiful conditions that rim-racked the churches of Asia Minor as is indicated by his servant John in the Book of Revelation. What the break with Judaism lost and what the church needs to regain is difficult to ascertain and perhaps could be the thesis of a detailed study; however, the purpose of this chapter is not to supply the missing link but to *describe* the mental attitudes that have flooded the church concerning public worship since those first crisis-filled days.

The description of most churches today should be the "church audience," and the average Christian even refers to the congregation in its public gathering as the audience. They are there to *hear, observe* and *criticize,* as did those first critics of Paul at Corinth.

Are there some legitimate reasons for this misconception? The answer is a truthful "yes." Each generation of church people grows up in the tradition of observing the routine of worship in the public gathering at eleven o'clock on Sunday morning and many of them return again that night for a vesper or evening preaching hour. The architecture of most church sanctuaries is more suited for the audience mentality than the sanctuary concept, which is desired by all clear thinking and serious students of worship, but is hard to realize. Every feature of the sanctuary of most churches is conducive to the audience mentality. The building is in a rectangular shape with the back row of pews or seats further away from the minister than what is called the front pew. Instead of the church gathering to worship, the church gathers to gaze!

There is a platform that is elevated so all can observe every movement from beginning to end. The minister sits in full view of the group and awaits his time to come forward. The platform has a pulpit in the center or on the side, which is the same symbolism of the "front and center stage" idea and sometimes a spotlight has been used to focus on the one requiring the group's attention. In the cult revival campaigns, the evangelist comes to the platform at a later time than the choir and music director. He makes his entrance on cue and sometimes a spotlight hits him as he enters. One man who was a "giant of a preacher" by reputation used to come into his church at a given time and kneel and pray under the focus of a spotlight. The platform architecture has been responsible for the continuation of the audience mentality to some extent.

Another phase of the audience overtone is the silence of the congregation as to outward contribution. About all any group offers is a response to the scriptural division of public reading and lusty "Amens" in the more vocal and emotional churches. Any way one chooses to look at the setting, it is the same as a movie theater or any other public performance of arts and crafts.

Added to this is the overemphasis on personal dynamics of the people leading the service. All who lead the ritual or order of service must be dynamic and gifted in public appeal, or else it is considered a dull hour and this emphasis on dynamic personal appeal is most magnified in the layman's mind. That the minister must have that something called color is as necessary to the average layman as his requirement that he be educated. In fact, it is safe to say that if a man has to depend on one without the other, he can go further on personal dynamism than on an adequate theological education.

Many in the younger generation of adults are most unhappy with older people coming into a beautiful place of worship and jabbering wildly before the service proper begins. They believe as Karl Barth that Christian worship is the most momentous, the most urgent, the most glorious action that can take place in human life. When one has the idea that he is congregated for *involvement and not situated for an attraction,* it makes a lot of difference. This change of mind-set could revolutionize Protestant Christianity. The main idea is to be involved, not to sit idly by and refuse to sing or meditate but to be involved and participate. People need to learn to judge the thought content of the sermon and to try to analyze just what the man is trying to say to them. Added with this is a continuous prayer for him as he delivers his message. There must be the feeling that the worshipper has a brother before him who needs the strength of his prayers, not an audience of spectators. If a man can't sing, he can make an attempt at reading the words. Most anything he does to offset the audience mentality will aid the pastor.

We have it and it is likely here to stay—this audience mentality—and it is as deeply ingrained in the attitude of the people as are many other traditions of their religious experience. In fact, the attitudes that make up the audience mentality are so interwoven with the average layman's grasp of his faith that it might well be impossible to untangle the threads lest he have much of the garment left at all.

At least a look at this maze of ideas and attitudes will be worth one's time. There are dozens of characteristics to this mentality at eleven o'clock, but a starter will be the fellow who comes into the building, sits down and leans back in a satisfied pose of comfort where he then begins to look around. If this is a woman spectator she is busy observing hats, clothing and other apparel. There is never a thought of a moment of private prayer or meditation and he or she may even nod at people, wave at a few and if one is a politician, this is a good time to sit in a most conspicuous place. This type person can tell who is at church and who is not and a good deal of his time is spent wondering where certain people are and why they are not present.

Many people of this vintage sit toward the back of the building. One noted author and speaker told of two men who came into the service and sat behind a curtain that had been drawn toward the back to make the small group feel more togetherness because the building was so large. These two men couldn't stand involvement so they sat on the far side of the drawn curtain and peeked around into the aisle the entire service. This illustration tells a lot about the attitude either consciously or unconsciously held by the person who constantly sits on the back seat. He is symbolizing his desire to retain his independence and he does not want to get involved. This back seat person wants to sit where he can view all the other people. He wants to observe them if controversy appears so he can play it safe and this tells him which side to choose should sides be drawn. He does not want to have to commit himself without first seeing what the others will do, therefore he is a good politician. The only problem with this characteristic is that public worship or public lectures are not the places where the Christian needs to play the politician's role. These back seat people will always be this way because of their inner attitudes toward the entire service. They are the non-involved!

The non-involved mentality is probably a majority complex in the average church service where few people get involved in any worship hour. The people who sit closer to the front are the more involved people as a rule and they are also the less critical normally. The seating of people in church tells more than the average layman thinks in a depth approach to group attitudes. These back seat critics are playing it safe so that they can slip out of the service in mind or body and no one will notice their absence.

Some of these non-involved critics visit first one church and then another never identifying with one group or church in their town because they do not want to be responsible for participation. They like to go and hear different preachers so they say. This way they can feel a sense of false objectivity that further enforces their attitude of the critical onlooker. They put a nominal sum in the offering plate and this is the price of admission to them. The support of the total church program is not important and to them it is as though they have come to the weekly floor show of the religious institution and have paid the price. Thus they are free to be like the Monday morning armchair quarterback. They criticize the music, the selection of hymns, the failure of the choir to do as they expected and last of all is the criticism of the preacher of the hour. He was too long, too drab, too emotional, not emotional enough, too loud, too quiet, or a dozen other analyses of a critical nature. These are the people who claim to be ecumenical in spirit but in reality are related to nothing of value and belong to the ever-growing group of passer-by critics.

One commentary on this group that needs injecting here is that it includes many of the younger set and appears to be intellectual and sophisticated. They believe in the overall goodness of the church's mission but want to observe the various clergymen at work before they will settle down to one routine. They are in reality "preacher shoppers." They will *never* identify with one group because they like the freedom from involvement and dearly enjoy the license to criticize because they can thus be more "objective," so they reason.

Sometimes there is the statement offered to a minister by one of this group that goes like this, "I will come over and hear you sometime." This is supposed to be the highest compliment the pastor can be paid. To think that each Sunday he will have some of this group before him is supposed to make him bubble with joy. To the deeply rooted pastor it causes a sense of sickness for this most corrupt attitude toward worship.

The audience mentality can be brought closer to the problems of the local pastor by the reference to some more of the church's critics who are with him all of the time. It is wished by some that these *would* go occasionally and visit other situations, hoping that it could broaden their outlook. Some of these critics in the "audience" each Sunday want the *ever new* by way of Scripture interpretation and preached word. They are dissatisfied with anything they have heard before and are suspicious of anything that smacks of age. They want their pastor to preach on the latest news release and they want a commentary of world events at every service. To them the Christian Scripture is for another world and another day. If they do hear the Scripture, they insist that there be no rehashing of Biblical scenes or ideas unless it is with a new twist. They just "don't get anything out of it" unless it is novel and previously unheard-of. This has given birth to some weird ideas with which some preachers have contrived to try to satisfy this craving for the unusual.

What the average layman doesn't realize is that it is almost next to an earthly impossibility for a man to come up with something sparkling and invigoratingly fresh each week and certainly not two or three times a week. This demand for fresh ideas is one of the contributing reasons men are rapidly leaving the pastoral ranks. There was a day when people did not have television and so many vivid means of bringing a new set of fresh ideas to the average man. The preacher on Sunday usually told the only news the people had all week but this is not true today. The high quality of production of news and the reproduction of what has been known is a threat to the parish pastor. Many of his people are dissatisfied with his retelling of any phase of Biblical life, and most assuredly what he will say has been said in one way or another for hundreds of years. This pressure to produce something new and original is just too much to bear. It is greatly increased by the audience mentality of "here I sit, tell me something I have not heard before," or "here I sit, tell me something I have heard before but you better make it better than I ever heard." No preacher can compete with the quality of preparation and production of a television release, yet the people unconsciously expect this of him!

What pastor has not experienced the day when he felt that he had some good points that were fresh and inviting? Then the next service the crowd would be noticeably up in numbers. The poor preacher sees the crowds come for more but he just can't "entertain" each time or be at his best as he was in the service before.

While some critical onlookers want the ever new, some want the *ever old*. They are suspicious of anything new and can immediately recognize it, so they think. Shockingly enough, their only criteria is their own experience and some things are certainly not new but the critic is so convinced because he has never heard it before that he thinks it was just sprung on him all at once. One pastor tells of an attempt at harmonizing the resurrection narratives of Mary Magdalene's synoptic appearances and the account in the Gospel of St. John of her visit to the empty tomb. Two elderly men protested openly in this discussion group, declaring that there *was no problem.* The pastor wisely and bravely answered that scholars had been wrestling with the problem for over fifteen hundred years and he didn't intend that their meeting that night should simplify the case with that one most unobjective statement.

The audience mentality includes this most dangerous group to learning, the lovers of the ever old. They feel that pastors are at their best when they use cliches and pious platitudes and they find comfort and security in hearing these ideas. It is to their disadvantage that most of this group make no effort to study. They make a pretense of study but their books and mental approach are grade-school in their level of attainment. These folks make one serious error that has caused more grief than any other one aspect of the people of God. They refuse to hear the prophetic word. There is so little said in most pulpits that is fresh and stimulating that it should behoove the laymen to appreciate any attempt at a new look at old problems and even if the pastor happens to be controversial, he should not be penalized. He is truly a man in a goldfish bowl in this area and that is where these people want him. They want to tie him to mouthing traditional ideas with the threat of losing his job. God had chosen to speak through the prophets of old and they were truly controversial. That a man is controversial is no bad mark. It *could be* the one distinguishing mark of a Christian minister in *some* given situations.

The lovers of the ever old have a great characteristic in common with the first century Pharisees; they are both lovers of tradition. They would stifle light and truth as quickly as they see it, especially if the light comes in new windows, and the truth is rejected if it is couched in new terminology. They are sometimes more interested in the way a thing is done than in the truth that is represented. This yen for traditional patterns of worship and preaching has stifled the church more than one would like to think. In fact, if a thing is done the same way *twice* it becomes a sacred tradition in the life of many churches. The tradition lover likes to see the machine running the same way all the time. He can spot any deviation in the pastor's sermon manner and routine. If the pastor varies his ideas to lean toward even the possibility of controversy, this type of person pricks up his ears and is ready to set himself with a closed mind for the rest of the sermon or to nurture open hostility toward the pastor. He thinks that preaching is a continuous flow of proclaiming the old truths. This type of person is normally most insecure in his religious life. He wants to hear the same things over and over in order to strengthen his ideas and he is most afraid of investigation into his presuppositions.

At this point there needs to be some light thrown on the

great difference in the pattern of teaching and preaching today and the pattern of these functions in the early church. Most laymen and clergymen think that preaching is to be identified by the vociferous proclamation of time-honored truths. This is best seen when the great doctrines of the church are declared in a stirring manner. While this may be so today and generally understood as preaching at its best, it is *just the opposite* on the part of the first preachers of the new covenant. This contemporary style is to proclaim *old* truths. When a man is prepared to articulate *new* ideas, he sets himself for a small group and is generally in a classroom situation. The contemporary description of what he is doing is called teaching. In other words, preaching today is a proclamation of the old, and teaching is the attempt to get the new and untried idea across to the hearer.

In the days of the first preachers of the resurrection-fact, the preacher was producing the heretofore unknown. The first preachers were exhorting people to faith in Jesus of Nazareth, the first to burst the bonds of death in resurrection. This new and exciting message caused *controversy, confusion, all kinds of dilemma and decision.* Crisis upon crisis came as a result of these revolutionary ideas and these preachers were even said to have "turned the world upside down." The teaching method was employed to train the new converts in the old covenant prophecies and to show their fulfillment in Jesus. In other words, if a distinction can be placed on the method and style as to content, the *first* preaching was a proclamation of the *new* and the *early* teaching was to restate it and undergird it with the old familiar ideas only giving them a Christian interpretation. While this can be considered a nebulous idea at first glance, it does give enough light to show the audience mentality and the reversal of these methods today.

Today the assembled crowds come to hear a man state the old truths from Sunday to Sunday and he is judged as a good preacher if he can "dress it up and make it exciting." When a man has something different, controversial, and that which borders on the need for real thought, he does not present it from the pulpit. His official board will tell him that the pulpit is *no place* to try new ideas and new interpretations. He is to say these things in smaller groups. Basically it is thought that the congregational gathering is not to learn the new and challenging, but there the preacher is to proclaim the familiar. Consequently, the idea of preaching and teaching is in *reverse order* today from the first century.

Also, preaching is considered as such according to its style. When a man is thundering away he is preaching and when he is in a conversational tone he is teaching. To the average layman content has nothing to do with it. Many men have had the embarrassing moment when after sermon delivery some people say that they would make good teachers, which means they are not entertaining enough, and in the same services others will say that they would make good preachers if they keep on trying, or if they learn to get louder and use more platitudes. Perhaps this one great reversal can offer a ray of light as to the reason why so much preaching today is so dull and uninteresting. Maybe the preacher needs to incorporate more of the unknown and to give the idea that he is forging new avenues of experience. This can of course go to the extreme, but real preaching is stimulating and *causes crisis. It brings forth a sword and sets a fire.* It can be said with almost certainty, that the average layman with his love for tradition and his disdain for the pastor who "rocks the boat" would not recognize valid New Testament preaching *if he heard it.*

The reversal of ideas of today and the first century as to teaching and preaching is one of great interest when pursued thoroughly. People don't want to be stirred to think at worship. This is a time for soothing ideas, certainly not a time for the proclamation of critical issues. Of course, the answer is offered by many that they *do* preach for decision and preach for commitment, but this they do to the unchurched individual. This goes a long way but does not approximate the need of the hour in the pulpit. There is a pressing need to wake up the "churched" who sit smugly in their nests each Sunday and the man in the goldfish bowl needs to get out and be given the opportunity to make the church member think. However, this is the one great thing people don't want to do at eleven o'clock. At a study club, perhaps so, but in the assembled congregation, no! Someone has said that the time of the least thought in all the week is at eleven o'clock on Sunday morning. Perhaps a genuine study of the role of first century preaching would give some needed boost to our lifeless pulpits.

So one dominant group of people that make up the audience mentality are the lovers of tradition. They like to see the machine of their church run smoothly, and quickly tell their minister that he is drawing a good salary and all the folks like him so why should he hazard his security by "getting out of line." They tell him that "things are not done overnight so why not relax and feed the flock." They say that the young pastor can distinguish himself as a mature individual if he will stay with the old truths and this threat that he will show himself to be "immature" is a real one to the young pastor. He is torn between allowing his young energetic mind the freedom it demands, or immediately joining the cult and getting into the time-worn paths. People like to be entertained on Sunday and they do not like to have to think. As one man so succinctly put it, "I work hard all week and I am worn out. I'll be hanged if I want to go to church and get all upset on Sunday morning. I want to at least relax in that hour."

The audience mentality has never had a stronger defender than the person who sits on the edge of his seat and dares the preacher to say something a little "modern or liberal." This person fits many categories of mental illness (to lesser degrees, to be sure), and furthermore he does not want his world blown apart. He will not be able to adjust so he sets himself in a rigid stand for the defense of what he considers orthodoxy and this simply means that he will not entertain anything new.

It is wondered when these individuals first stopped thinking. When they declare that they have heard a thing a certain way all their lives, *it is just not so.* Every man is born naked in body and in mind. There is a time when each individual hears words and ideas for the first time. It was *then* that he gave himself to these ideas and patterns of thought. Just where along the way did he decide to quit thinking and draw the door shut to any more new light? If it is agreed that a baby comes into the world with an open mind, then it must be agreed that that same mind is deliberately closed somewhere along in its development. This being true, it is ostensible that any person could have believed a lie "all his life."

It is of the greatest necessity that in the world of ideas, particularly religious ideas, that a man or woman have an open mind to check and give counterchecks to his thoughts. The individual is deceiving himself in the most absurd manner when he refuses new experiments into truth because he was not born with his ideas. Someone gave them to him and he believed them and for the most part never checked them out for himself. *That someone could have been wrong!*

Our Lord Jesus made a startling statement that for the most part is overlooked. Matthew, in the thirteenth chapter and the fifty-second verse, records him as saying, "Therefore every scribe which is instructed unto the kingdom of heaven is like unto a man that is an householder, which bringeth forth out of his treasure things new and old." In other words no man has a treasure of thought worth having unless out of it comes the *new* and invigorating as well as the old. This new he is to bring out is not the absurd and spectacular as we have seen some people desire. It is nevertheless new and rich for the people who will hear him speak.

All good preachers instructed in the life of Christ and the new covenant will have *something* to say. *Many pulpits are best characterized as having nothing to say.* Some people walk up to the pastor and tell him that they liked his sermon because he agreed with them but this is no indication that anything of real importance has been said. To speak meaningfully, a man must use speech methods of parable, sarcasm, humor and other ways to *force* the man who has the audience mentality into the role of the congregational mentality, the role of involvement in the whole scope of the presentation of the gospel. So much for the traditionalists.

The audience mentality is further seen in the transfer of people from one church to another. Here the newcomer is sometimes the severest "audience" critic. Back where he came from in River City his pastor did it this way or that way and was "highly successful" and he just doesn't like what amounts to the change of theater seats. He likes the church he came from best because the show was better and he is determined that when this pastor leaves he will recommend the "performer" back home. If these people could just see the preachers he has seen, so he thinks, the whole hour would be enlivened. He is the layman who has all the answers because he has known a pastor who has had "the keys to the kingdom." There are only a few of these people in any church but they create much unrest.

Many a good woman has been ruined because she worked as a part-time church secretary. She has been on the "inside of the show" and this has made her a critic from backstage forevermore. She never thinks of worship, but thinks of seeing that the show is run as she witnessed it before so she thunders into the church office with the "I've been on the inside routine and if you need me call on me. I can help you put it over." Or there is the big contributor who thinks that because he gives more than the average man he deserves a greater say, so he too cues from backstage. He sits in a conspicuous place and directs the proceedings from behind the scenes yet gives the impression that he is a most humble man. He is best seen in the board meetings, not in church. The church service is a big production to these people. They have had experiences of "operating" a church before and are well qualified to set it properly in motion now.

Sunday morning at eleven o'clock would not be complete without the "mood" group. They are made up of those folks who come once in a while as the mood strikes them and brag about the "roof not crashing in." They are really proud of their lack of consistent attendance. One gets the impression that God himself should shake a cloud or two when these august people come into His presence. They walk down to the front, usually after the service starts and find a seat. The show can continue. There was no weekend trip to take, no athletic event that interested them and so they can "make the scene" in church this Sunday. "Didn't you see me?" they say to the pastor the next day. "Aren't you proud of me?" they say. The poor guy has to preach to these people who are in the "mood."

These people who come once in a while blow hot and cold. They may even come several Sundays in a row, especially around revival time when the cult evangelist arrives. They really go for that guy. If it is August he will serve as inspiration until the football season starts. Now, these people are in no mood for serious thought and they are in a kindred relationship to that great spectator critic who comes and seems to take exception to everything the luckless parson says. He finds fault all the way through the sermon. However, he is a real critic at *every* public event. It is not that he is faulting the pastor necessarily, it is that he is just a fault finder. These are hard cases for the troubled soul in the pulpit to have to look at. Some of the sourest faces sit and sing lustily, "Oh Happy Day."

Then there is the person who is a nervous wreck. This is the longest stretch she has to endure without coffee or a cigarette. Some of these folks want a soothing performance. They differ from those who want a traditionally soothing hour because they have no interest in ideas new *or* old. They just want an hour's haven for jangled and tangled nerves. Surely things can go smoothly for them in church, so they think, so there they sit for a type of false therapy. Extra thought would give them a rash, so they want a quiet unemotional service, please. Right across the aisle, however, is the character who demands the "whip it up routine." Life is one dull moment after another and he wants to see his preacher preach as if he were fighting a swarm of bumblebees.

It was said of Abraham Lincoln that this was his idea of preaching but this is rather doubtful. These people want a superb performance with great portions of the congregation catching what is usually called in theological circles, hell! They want to see the rich castigated and the rowdy youth threatened with the loss of any virtue he might have left. They are "honest," however, and desire that their own toes be stepped on. In fact, they are the ones mentioned earlier who don't feel that they have been to church unless they get "hit" or their toes stepped on. They come out of the service and remark joyfully just how their feet ache and this is supposed to offer some valid proof to the preacher that he has had good audience response. Sometimes the fellow in question is not quite so honest and declares, "He really let *them* have it today, didn't he!"

Closely akin to this ticket bearer is the person who wants to feel so whipped and browbeaten that he or she can have what is known as a spiritual catharsis. He wants to go, feel bad, then feel washed and go on his way to do as he jolly well pleases. It becomes an end in itself and it all takes place right there in the service. Catholics have been criticized most unfairly for confessing and then going out and doing as they please, but the Protestant in mind here is guilty of the same thing he accuses the Catholic brother of doing. He would stoutly deny the resemblance but to the astute observer of guilt psychology this is exactly what happens. This is the person who continually confesses his failures and sometimes he is chronic about walking down the aisle and rededicating himself. He is a pathetic person, to be sure, and badly in need of a deeper understanding of group worship and personal psychology. Endless "altar calls" for rededication are *harmful* and their number should be drastically reduced. They exploit too many of these who are susceptible to this sort of thing.

Another of the mood group is the person who is tired and not in control of his emotions because he has made no genuine preparation for worship. He just barely gets to the service by the time it starts or just as the "curtain goes up." He just sits there and is rather surprised when he is moved in any capacity because his wife made him come, or in the case of a woman, she felt it was her duty to go and "surely he could accompany her." She is worn out from getting the children ready and a little put out with him because all he did was sleep later than she and read the paper with his second cup of coffee. So they both get there just under the wire, with no preparation in prayer or meditative concern to meet God. They would be the most surprised if anything of real consequence happened at eleven o'clock other than a deep breath when they fall into the pew. They even resent standing for hymns; the show could go on without all this standing, they think.

Another most interesting group with this audience mentality is the group that comes for social respectability. They go to all the good events, the best operas, the best movies, plays and outdoor events and they are most interested in the esthetics of the place. After all, it is a restful and beautiful atmosphere because there is ample weather conditioning and comfortable pews and the lighting is perfect. They get that good feeling from having gone and will frankly state that it just makes a fellow feel better to go to church on Sunday. When they miss, they just don't feel as good. This is really no genuine test of Christian discipleship or attribute. A person can miss a meal and not feel as good either.

Sometimes these people are prone to show off their church service. They have visitors at times and certainly want them to come to church with them to hear the choir and hear their pastor. Of course, they call the pastor if they know him well enough and tell him to get a cracker-jack sermon ready because they are going to have guests and they have been telling them what a good preacher he is so they don't want to be embarrassed by his getting off on a tangent of new ideas and stirring everyone up. These folks sit as tightly wound up as can be for fear something will go wrong. Immediately after the service they say to their guests, "Well, how did you like it? Great, wasn't it?" One can hear the same question in front of a movie theater.

Selling the service to visitors wouldn't be complete without the insistence that they join the church. This competitive bid for members on the basis of the flair of the service is not unusual. One of the "come-ons" in a larger town where there are as many as two churches of the same denomination (or this idea can cross denominational lines) is to "sell the service" as a means of attracting people. Now if they are newcomers with wealth and rank, the pastor is advised that they will be in the service and to be sure and get to shake their hands as soon as the service is over. The sale must be made! The people have done their part, now the pastor had better produce. The "come hear our preacher" group would do better to consider that this approach borders more on the theatrical than the spiritual. When one minister stated rather categorically at the conclusion of the service that he was not interested in merely adding new members by transfer, there were gasps from some of the wives of the elders. How in the world can they face these people at the bridge club if there is no concentrated effort on the part of their pastor to "sell their church"?

The most vividly hypocritical phenomenon of the audience mentality is the one of using little children in programs; every pastor has seen this used in many ways. People will come out to a congregational meeting to see their children "perform" who will not come out at other times. It seems wonderful that parents will do this, but only the more perceptive see the danger. *What is this saying to children?* It is saying that their fathers or mothers are not interested in the regular routine of worship and a real blow is struck at the heart of worship. A parent who will not bring his child faithfully to regular worship and who comes for children's choirs or dramatic programs is lending the worst possible influence to his child and many of these children are not brought to church unless they "perform." This damages their understanding of the real purpose of the service and this is a use of the church for the satisfaction of parents' or grandparents' needs. Worse than this is the fostering at an early age of the audience mentality within the child. Perhaps the greatest sin is the one of sham on the part of adults who come out to "kiddie" programs but *will not raise those same children* in regular periods of worship. The child unconsciously thinks that church, like everything else, is built around him, therefore he gets started in his training all wrong. Father is a Christian and so is Mother, so they say, but they seldom come unless little Johnny performs so the child suffers most from this shallowness of spirituality.

The audience mentality finds a welcome component in the choir and organist who join some pastors in grandstanding. At this point the choirmaster talks of the "performance" next Sunday and the organist also thinks in terms of Sunday's performance. She moves all over the organ bench to show just how difficult it is to whip this creature and to bring it into subjection for the smooth-as-silk offertory, which is sometimes a way-out selection and as far from the spirit of a Christian worship service as dinner music; however, she is playing for the few who can understand and recognize the selection. This is her private performance and she wrestles that noisy creature to the ground and slides breathlessly off the bench after her show is over.

Then there is the grandstanding soloist. Sometimes this is a young person whose father has called the church office to indicate that his daughter will be home from college and that she has just given a recital and he would like for her to do one of the numbers for the congregation (or audience).

Last of all our hero himself, the preacher, takes over. After all, he has the featured spot on the program. Often the crowd is so remote or spellbound by the music that he must break the spell and get the attention for himself, so he does the most absurd—he tells a joke!

This platform compliment to the spectator layman sets the perfect stage for the spectator complex and the average layman as well as pastor thinks that the service is to bring about a religious demonstration. Even one idle bystander at the cross of our Lord wished for a religious demonstration when he said to the mob that apparently Jesus was calling for Elijah and then added that he would like to see Elijah come and take Jesus down from the cross.

Now, when some of these spectators go out of the service without the desired results, they are heard to say the most dreadful words a pastor can hear: "I didn't get anything out of the service today!" Other spectators say just the opposite, "He really had it today, didn't he?" It is much like the golfer who is able to stay in the fairway and on another occasion just does not have the feel. Some say that the preacher is getting better all the time or he was better than last Sunday or, conversely, he was not up to par today or the morning message was better than the night. It makes no difference how it is sized up, *many contemporary church services are spectator events as much as any other acknowledged spectator event in our modern culture!*

This is largely the fault of the pastor because he has succumbed to these faulty and secular attitudes. People demand a show and he gives it to them; many men design the entire church organization to come to a focus in this one service. Instead of the Sunday service being one phase of the work of the community of believers, it is the focus of attention. Everything rises or falls on the way it "goes over." The audience mentality is strangely shared by most pastors, especially those of the cult development. By and large the church congregation meets once or twice a week to see the machine in operation and that is just about all there is in the way of a functioning body.

In these services the music and other activities prior to the preaching are termed "the preliminaries," which lead up to the main event and his spot on the show. Everything is to focus on him. It *is true* that all should be in a harmonious arrangement of thought. It is *not true* that what precedes the sermon is just a preliminary to the main event. In many services everything hinges on the response to the sermon, usually during a period of invitation. One pastor was overheard to exclaim his wonder. He was amazed at how an evangelist just seemed to stand and bow his head after he had preached and the people came streaming forward during the invitation. The pastor concluded that the evangelist "had it." That a few of the prominent evangelists have a genuine urgency is not denied at all, but it *is* denied that they have any key to God's conviction of sinners any more than any other dedicated man. In fact, with the tremendous psychological buildup of their campaigns and the effective work in getting them before the people at the right time, they could sell anything at these meetings and have success.

In some church services the pastor's people that have gathered for preaching have learned to adjust to the service the way he desires. Many times he can turn on the emotion and turn it off. It's like the little girl who walks out to the rest room during the sermon and walks back in time to come forward during the invitation at the insistence of the pleading minister. Great care should be taken in these appeals so that the more emotional people will not be exploited. However, many pastors *want to do just that*! One mother tells of her son who in his earlier years was so sorry for the pastor when no one responded to his invitation that he always wanted to go forward in order to make the preacher feel better. The real highlight of the hour is whether or not any "moves" will be made and if no one comes forward the service is usually considered of no real value. The pastor starts questioning himself as to what could be wrong with his own heart that God would not bless him with visible results. Some of the most un-Christian methods and ways of dealing with people take place during the invitations every Sunday. The "then or never" threat is not for the person's sake but for the preacher's ego many times!

This is a serious threat to any genuine understanding of the preached word and the Holy Spirit's work of continuous blessing on that word. This idea has the Holy Spirit or God or however one phrases the heavenly intervention as the "great manipulator of the moment." This discounts His previous dealings with individuals and His continuous dealings with them after the service is over. In fact, some people tell of being in services and observing when "it hit him or her like lightning" and they can attest to another person's conversion because they were there and witnessed it. They tell of great moments of tears and contrition. Sometimes these I-got-religion people are not linked with Christ's people today. They think that the important thing is that they were *really dealt with* in a real "live" service sometime in the past.

Some pastors see this service as a test of their ability to produce and in reality it is something they need for reassurance. Many men are hard to live with if they can't count

converts after they have preached. This is like the pastor
who had been in ninety-one revivals and had converts to
his message in all but the last one. He told this congregation about his previous "success" with reaping and that he
was going back to his home and pray that God would show
him what there was in his life that "clogged" up the drain
from heaven's power to his preaching. Now these ideas are
found in supposedly educated churches and the reader
would be missing the truth of these sordid evaluations of
preaching if he thought that this type of thing only went
on in the lower class of church life. Some of the largest
"First" churches have a diet of this each week! The audience response is a necessary part to many pastor's need for
the validity of their messages. They must be continually
told, by the symbol of visible results to their pleadings, that
God is with them. Elmer Gantry is reincarnated at this
point thousands of times in America each Sunday.

It is also their proof to their congregations that they still
have what it takes. They are like the old sheriff who can
still shoot straight and who wants the townspeople off his
back. Many a frantic cult pastor has had an evangelist in
to give a needed moral boost and to get "something going"
in the way of converts in order for the pastor to prove to
his congregation that he still has what it takes. The layman
is not suspicious but this is why the evangelist makes a
little speech about how fortunate the church is to have
such a man. He is purely and simply mending fences and
the more astute pastor at manipulating the congregation

for his own ends can shift gears in his sermon to coincide with the crowd in attendance. He can get an inspiration from the people to give thoughts he has not prepared. The response during the invitation is the one great moment of truth for him and sadly enough for many of his people. The audience mentality has saturated every phase of these services of "worship."

No discussion of this type approach to worship would be complete without what this author considers to be the lowest point to which churches can stoop. This is the reference to the worship service being used to attract people, or to validate the Christian faith, by the use of "big name people." Graham R. Hodges, a Congregational minister, had a clever article in the *Pulpit Digest* in which he pointed out the use of big names in pulpits. He wrote, "Because . . . great persons seek help from the minister, the Church is really coming up in the world. Once it catered mainly to dirty fishermen, carpenters, and sail makers. Now, first vice-presidents and senators seek its help. What more proof is needed to show that God is finally making the grade?" These people are being used and are in return using the church with its lofty purposes for their own craving for recognition and new experience. As one professional actor said to another, "You haven't *seen* an audience unless you get to speak to a church group. You really get attention there."

There are several categories of notables that some pastors use. The athlete would be a good starter for purposes of discussion here. It occurs when some athlete who has attained stardom or some kind of national recognition is brought into the service to "give his testimony." Some of these young men are most sincere but the fact that they are All-American should have no bearing on their use in a service; this smacks of the floor show routine in the worst way. Sometimes these boys are good boys, but not especially good or even professing Christians. They speak in a general way of God on their side, that they prayed before each game, or that God's the real coach of life, and other pat phrases. Usually this draws a large crowd and what is suggested, and it is at this point that it is most distasteful, is that *now* the Christian faith can be considered genuine, workable and worthy of acceptance by the young people because this great athlete believes in it and "look where God has put him." (Jesus Christ has never needed the validation of any great or notable person.) Sometimes entire athletic teams are honored at a church service and this becomes a syncretism of Christ and culture that is completely pagan in its core.

Another group that is represented in the "testimony" category (which continues to add to the audience mentality) is the converted movie star or performer in another part of the arts and sciences. Big ads are bought in the paper to advertise the person and to tell of the service at which he is to be the featured "giver of the personal testimony." Any identification the star has with the church is acceptable to most pastors of this vintage. These pastors want a crowd and want to identify themselves with notable people. The idea is that surely if God can clean up a movie star's life he can work on most any local sinner.

This would not be a sufficient criticism if some reference were not made to the politician who is a loyal and devoted church member. He is invited to give his testimony to show how you can be a Christian in politics. Or there is the beauty queen who gets the first offer to come to churches in order to show the young girls that one can be pretty and at the same time be a Christian. Sometimes pastors have been mortally embarrassed by developments following these testimonies in relation to the beauty queen and to nature. This type of pastor wants just anyone who has gained fame and fortune in the entertainment world because this will assure him of a crowd and that is uppermost in his mind and heart and is exactly what he wishes for. Also, men with money have been paraded across the stage or from behind a pulpit to declare how God will make a man rich if one begins to tithe. Now the harsh reality of the matter is that in each case presented above, if that same person were not important for other reasons, he *would not be important for his testimony*! Who ever heard of a pastor asking his janitor to give his testimony or of a scrubwoman to give hers. After all, they have tithed for twenty-five years, but how does one explain their vocation? Where is God in their lives?

The Christian faith does not need the theatrical or the testimony of *anyone* for it to be genuine and meaningful

in the life of any man. Ralph W. Sockman placed worship
at its highest level of meaning when he wrote, "Every
seventh day the church in her worship calls us around in
front of the loom to look at the pattern on which we have
been working. She bids us compare the design of our days
with the pattern shown us in the Mount of Sinai and the
Mount of the Beatitudes. Thereupon we feel impelled to
cut some threads and to pull others more tightly, and most
of all we renew the picture of the whole plan. The symbols,
the songs, the ritual, and the messages of worship help us
to repossess ourselves of the certitudes which were ours in
the fleeting moments of flashing insights and to reillumine
the common day by the meditative recovery of the celes-
tial light."

This business of the big name attraction at a church or
a service "honoring" football teams or fraternal organizations is to prostitute the power of God in exchange for
nothing more than the sensual desire of people to be entertained. The audience mentality is of an exceedingly complex nature and one of the worst results of this mentality
is that people will not join into the spirit of praying. They
just listen or think of something else while one is praying
and some will not even sing the hymns. Our church services must become a time for worshiping congregations
not houses for attendants at a spectator-event situation.
Often it is heard from some individuals such statements as,
"I go only for the preaching" or "I just go for the music."
All of these ideas are bred as a result of this complex

confusion as to the role of the person in the pew at eleven o'clock. Perhaps to be made aware of this would inspire some pastors and dedicated laymen to start a cleansing of the motives in both the pulpit and pew. Both are equally guilty and one breeds the response in the other!

5

The Courage to Be Genuine

Should a minister start speaking his mind or leave the parish ministry as hundreds of young pastors are doing every year?—LOUIS CASSELS

The pastor is certainly a man in a goldfish bowl and he is there because many people want to keep him there where he can perform, look good, entertain, go in circles, always be there when one needs to look in, but cannot get out. It must be said that *he is* getting out! Scores every week are getting not only out of the bowl but out of the water because the ranks are being depleted probably faster than in any other profession.

There are some very conscientious men who do not want out of the water but do want out of the bowl. The churches must do an about-face in just about every area of concern. They must interest young men for the pastoral ministry and people should not kid themselves, because there is one reason and only one real and primary reason young men are not responding to this high calling. *They have seen too much in local churches* where they have witnessed the high office of the pastorate being turned into that of a "sublime tinkerer." The pastor is a harried, pressed, frustrated and much maligned individual and he has been forced to assume every duty from helping the janitor to counseling in areas he knows nothing about. He is like many rivers, a mile wide and an inch deep and as such, few young men want to tackle the job and go to school the seven years or longer required to get an earned divinity degree.

There must then be a redefining of the office. The pastorate must have a job description and this must be drawn up by the official board or the congregation. The pastor's authority must be spelled out. Where is he to make decisions and under what circumstances? He must know what his duties are as required by the congregation or the official board. These must be in print and available to the congregation. Under what conditions is he expected to visit the sick and when is he *not* under obligation? When he is under no obligation he needs to be made to feel that he is free of this strain of expectancy and just what each church demands is to be written out. The churches must have many, many business sessions in which the people as a body and to the last man go over the requirements expected of their pastor. There needs to be a wholesale approach to educating the congregations as to a strict and helpful definition of the pastoral office in *that* local church. This should be *binding on his people* as well as on the pastor. When these detailed ideas are ratified by the congregation, there should be discipline as to their adherence on both pastor and people.

His duties do not need to be specified as to a rigid schedule of time; that is his business. But as to his *overall function* in each field such as preaching, visiting and counseling, he should have a limit as to how entrenched this should be. His people as well as he should be forced by a sense of honor to abide by this limit and those people who talk detrimentally should be dealt with accordingly. A pastoral relations committee can be appointed and all grievances should go to this committee and never be voiced on the street. The committee should talk with the pastor and determine if he is failing the prescribed routine and job description set down by the congregation.

Pastor-congregation open forums should be held periodically to educate the pastor to the needs of his people and to educate the people to his predicament. The congregation needs to re-evaluate their understanding of the office. Problems that have been pressing on him should be brought to the group. He should feel free to ask for help or their patience. He can find a great source of strength in this group discussion if he will only set it up and try it. People have a way of being nicer than they think they can be when they have to stand on their feet and voice their compliments or complaints. These meetings should be the only time that honorable people criticize. This should be the time to "put up or shut up." If there is an insidiousness to a group and they will not discuss their grievances in the proper place and at the proper time, the congregation needs to further protect the pastor from these vicious tongues and in some way discipline the people. There is a way to put a stop to all the bickering in churches if the official boards are courageous men. It is unfortunate, however, that so often these very men are not honorable and they or their wives are responsible for much unrest through gossip.

The pastoral office needs a large dose of the respect that it once had. Why it is gone is not so very important; that there is very little genuine respect for the local pastor is sadly true. Respect can come from the fact that his job is impossible. Any man who will tackle it deserves a measure of respect and respect should come because it is a godly work he is doing. This ancient calling is ordained of God and has as its forebears the greatest names of literature and history. This position is filled by a man of God and he fails, is weak at times and all too human at other times, has his ups and downs and sins like any other man, but he is different; he is a man of God and God has set him apart for his noble work. He deserves the best of conversation about himself and his office does not need to be dragged through the mud of idle conversation. The youth do not need to hear their parents cruelly talking about the pastor's failures. The office is a high office and regardless of the man who fills it in the local church it is still the noble calling created nearly two thousand years ago in the early church.

We are in need of men with the courage to be as genuinely sincere as they desire the response of the churches to be toward them. This must begin by a true analysis of our recent past. Any assessment of our problems must analyze the rise and decline of church work since World War II and notice that decline is mentioned along with the rise because it is just that way. We are seeing a dedicated resistance to the church and the men who have become pastors during the great growth of church work are under the gun to do something about the indifference raging on all fronts.

The period beginning with the years following World War II is a significant period for every field of "investigation." Every area of life in America has undergone tremendous change. Science has accomplished more in this period than perhaps all the rest of the time in human history. A history of scientific study would not be complete without considerable attention given to this period because new achievements in the world of science have affected man tremendously. The field of education has also changed because schooling under the G.I. Bill offered college work to many people who would not have received it otherwise. More young people are enrolled in college today than ever before and media of communication have been fantastic. This is the era of television in which people can sit in their living rooms and behold more of the world in one night than their forefathers saw in a lifetime. This has been a time of economic boom in which big business has predominated. The small drug and grocery stores are being threatened by large chain concerns and new and magnificent buildings are rapidly replacing those which though adequate in the thirties are obsolete today. Only a few things have been pointed out and surely much else could be said about these years but this gives something of a background for the following remarks.

The churches have changed too, and new and impressive church buildings can be seen in just about every town or village. This has been an era of expansive (and expensive) church building. Religion has become a more important part of daily life, at least this is thought to be true by the rising statistics of church attendance. Because of the crisis of World War II many people found a genuine faith to live by, and immediately following those war years our churches could not accommodate the crowds. New buildings were built and many new churches formed.

However, before we get carried away with the rosy picture, we should look more realistically at the facts. First of all, these years saw the great move to urban areas. People left the rural areas during the war to find good employment in the cities. The vacancies needed filling where the younger men and women had left when they enlisted in the war effort. Defense plants, shipbuilding and ammunition factories drained the countrysides of prewar population.

Women whose husbands and fathers were in the service of their country gained steady employment in urban areas and when the war ended, only a small percentage of these people went back to their rural homes. Consequently, rural churches died by the hundreds almost overnight, giving a stimulus to urban church life that it had not known before. New churches sprang up in growing areas of the cities, and that is just the point, the churches emerged where the people went. Churches were seldom founded where the people *had been.*

On the surface this looked like a great religious awakening and while an awakening to some degree might have taken place, it still remains that underneath the surface of the thing the urban advance and the death of rural church life contributed much to the growth of churches. Another important factor is the rise of population, which simply means that we have more people now than ever before and churches have received their due proportion of this increase.

Probably most important was the great desire to get members. In some cases, competitive races were run between churches for membership gains. This means that some of our churches have grown for the same reason that chain stores have grown; the convenience of purchasing goods coupled with the lowering of prices has been the success story for many businesses. Church membership has been made convenient, acceptable in society, and in some cases, expected. Affiliation with a church, especially now that they are so prominently located on choice corner lots, is helpful and advantageous to men in their social and economic climb. A "disciplined church" is a thing of another day, thus our churches have grown, but so has big business and many fear it is because of *kindred reasons. Now, judgment has run hot on all of us.* A decline is seen by all and this is a realistic problem to the sincere pastor. What does all of this have to do with the pastoral ministry? Whatever involves churches involves the minister. During this time of urban church growth, the pastor has come in for unprecedented publicity. More than the pastor making the churches large (as is thought by many), the churches have made great names for their shepherds. The pastor has become in many cases a great administrator. Some men made great in this period could have never risen above a small town parish in any other era. Denominational publications, and especially periodicals such as the weekly papers, have served as sounding boards for the aggrandizement of men in "large" churches. Credit has been heaped upon these men for the ability to "build" churches. It reminds one of the story of the woodpecker out in Texas where it seems that this certain woodpecker was high atop a great tree, working like a riveter machine. Suddenly a bolt of lightning streaked across the sky and split the tree in half. It it said that that woodpecker has been telling to this day that it was he who split the tree.

Many of our contemporary church conventions are subtly used by "woodpeckers" who are continually telling about the splitting of trees. Have we not all heard about "Reverend Accomplished, that *great* pastor, of one of our *great* churches"? The truth is that the church is "great" because it is big and the pastor is a big name because the church is big. The mistaken thinking behind this emergence of the highly organized church is that the growth in this period was due to "effective organizational methods." It is the thinking of many that pastors have been deluding themselves and that it was not highly organized methods that caused our boom in church growth, but the factors mentioned earlier. This, of course, is a stunning blow to the ego of many men, but there is truth here.

However, peaks have been reached in many denominations, and methods that used to be almost sacred are now coming under serious scrutiny. A real decline in attendance is seen on the horizon and many denominational leaders are saying that the need is more organization. "Keep the people busy" is the watchword. The trouble with this thinking is that a church so highly organized will actually hinder home life instead of helping it. Most churches meet a minimum of three nights weekly and at least one organizational night for one or two members of the family. Now, more meetings are called for by some.

Another danger here is that the pastor will find his congregation divided because so many meetings will actually foster self-righteousness. People who have no other social outlet will find one in the many meetings of the church. Before long, this "faithful" group will be looking askance at the other people who are not at the church but are attending some other function. Since the church meeting has spiritual sanction and "spiritual" matters come first, then the other community functions are no less than "sinful" and attendance is "compromising with the world."

The pastor will find himself preaching to two different groups on Sunday morning, especially if he goes into (God forbid) a ten-minute period of announcements of the meetings of the forthcoming week where one group will sprout halos and the other group will be bored. This is not meant to be an over simplification, but a real problem that many have already experienced.

The Sunday morning service has been used by many pastors as a period of promotion for the activities of the following week. It is not uncommon to hear pastors preach parts or entire sermons on the need to attend some function that is forthcoming. There is a desperate need for a sense of worship to fill the Sunday morning service and the pastor is doing his people a disfavor when he uses the morning worship hour as a period of "marshaling his forces for the coming week's activities."

One of the problems that will arise as a result of minimizing activities will be a reaction from some of his people because many of his people like much activity. In fact, a church's contribution to the community is gauged by some as to the nights the facilities are used and the numbers that are posted as a visible sign of "going forward." The pastor will face trouble from this element, which has been using the church for social outlet under the guise of organizational loyalty. Christianity has been relegated to a Boy Scout type merit system with seals, awards, etc., given for attendance. If this element is strong in the church, the pastor will have a hard time doing little else but handing out awards.

In this period since World War II, many significant changes have made their way on to the American scene, but the rapid growth of churches has been a phenomenal thing. The pastor's rise to prominence in community life and his mistaken ideas as to what "builds" a church have dominated the church scene. Now the prominence is fading and there is only negligible growth. Genuine growth is certainly not questioned by anyone; however, many men have matured during this period and there is a frustration to maturity. Many men have gone through these days of great growth after the Second World War. What have the younger men inherited and what have the older men given birth to? We have witnessed both sides of the picture, one of great growth and one of genuine decline.

The pastor is the mediator between the renewal of the church philosophy and the people and the burden is on his shoulders. He must take and sift through the problems, suggestions, cures and questions in an effort to bring meaning to the church but he first must bring a new sense of meaning to his own calling. This period of unparalleled growth and decline of churches following the war has brought two pressing problems to the local pastor.

The first thing that is rather obvious is that the men who were responsible for the rapid growth are as frustrated as any group anywhere. They have seen the day finally come that their methods, manners and personal appeal are not doing what they used to do. The mighty have fallen and truly all pastors are sensing their feet of clay more than ever. Those who had all the answers of the successful pastorate ten years ago are now extremely concerned with the repudiation of the institutional church by some of the younger generation of adults. Where a man's father was faithful as a cultural habit, his son doesn't care the least about old conventions and the demanded discipline of church loyalty.

The other problem that a sharp rise and now the definite decline brings is one of ideological basis. The era of the hard sell and intensive promotion is gone for many men, yet their people, or a goodly number of them, have been born and fed on this quasi-theatrical, Madison Avenue type diet. *They have come to like it.* It is man-centered all the way. It emphasized big numbers, big buildings, big speakers—big, big, big. Their idea is for more of the same while some far-seeing people are convinced that this was never worthy of the Christian faith. It can be said with all candor that much of the unrest today is brought on by the superficiality of the church's outreach to the world in the years following the war. All the gimmicks have been used and people are not responsive to them in this enlightened and searching generation. Therefore, we must be good students of our past in order to be genuine in the future because some things must go because they are cheap and tawdry.

Also we must be genuine in our approach to Christian education. The typical "Micky Mouse" curriculum of Sunday school and the youth organizations must be abandoned, and the sooner the better. Millions of people have been enrolled in Bible study classes and never had a course in how the Book came to be in the first place. They rather think it came out of heaven on golden plates ready for type-casting. The night preaching service in churches that have it must give way to something better, first of all because it is dying in attendance anyway and it is better to rally what people there are left to a better use of the Sunday night time. Secondly, this is too much preaching and not enough teaching. No serious pastor can prepare adequately for this other service and one on Wednesday night also. The churches are sick of a steady Sunday night diet of three points and a sad story and the next generation will not come to hear this because they will have heard all the sad stories as children!

The one area of neglect is the youth. Yes, they have been given ample parties, Ping-Pong sessions and hayrides. What they have not been given is enough truth about the facts of the Bible and Christian history to save their faith when it is challenged in college or elsewhere. This is not a reflection on the colleges for destroying faith. If they can do so, and do not, someone somewhere else will do it. In any event the church has failed him.

The man in the goldfish bowl needs to be out of the rut of the night preaching service and he needs to teach. The average pastor of any size church at all is never face to face in a teaching capacity with his people. He delegates that to other people and the only time he sees them is to preach his outlines while the children write notes. There needs to be a real deep curriculum of study set up for the Sunday nights in the church. It should resemble a school with classroom effects where subjects of old and new can be taught, just anything but the memory verse attitude. Elton Trueblood mentioned this possibility when he wrote, "The congregation must, accordingly, be reconstructed into the pattern of a small theological seminary with the pastor as the professor." This writer's congregation has adopted this and we have met with a new sense of enthusiasm for learning.

Memory verses are good for younger children but for junior high and high school ages there needs to be something more solid in the way of history and reason. The pastor is the only one trained to do it and if he is tied down to the tradition of preaching to some old folks on Sunday nights, then the young people will continue to suffer. One day there will be no one left with the habit of Sunday evening attendance at all and the churches with this habit ought to *capitalize on it now* and change their curriculum and order of services. Most people will ignore these words but when a light bulb goes out it seldom gives more than a flicker of warning and then all is dark. It takes a long time to change the bulb in the dark.

The desire to be genuine must take into account the need to recall individuality. The pastoral office should be marked with the characteristics of a person who acts perfectly natural because God calls a man the way he is and he is to use that which is natural for him in the way of his talents. When a man is more concerned about being as other preachers to the detriment of his individuality, he greatly hinders what he can do for God and man. When the Scripture says that Jesus grew in favor with God and man this was the author's attempt at telling all the world what Jesus the Son of God was like as a young man—*he was natural.* The pulpit doesn't need more of the same. It is thirsting for *voices* in the wilderness of images and cult patterns. Paul Scherer clearly emphasized this in his Lyman Beecher Lectures when he said, "To be only yourself six days in the week and on the seventh to be no other, whether in reading the service or in preaching the sermon, may not be very thrilling; but it is the only hope there is for you."

A man should work hard at avoiding the cult patterns of voice tones, which sound as though he has a mouth full of mush, and of stereotyped mannerisms of doing and saying things. We must learn to live within the thought patterns of our world. Many men are still thinking in a nineteenth century approach to Christianity.

No truly genuine minister is lazy at study. Most men

have found that when they study hard and work hard they produce a better quality of ministry. *This became their security.* A man doing a good job need not be too concerned that he will be replaced. The ever fresh and invigorating mind of a thinking pastor will be all the security he needs. His people will rally to him and love him. Bishop Gerald Kennedy once wrote, "When your preaching shows the results of study, you will have the support of the congregation in reserving time for study." The preacher must guard against allowing the mood of the hour to dictate how he preaches. For this reason series preaching gives a man much more time to study and to guard against reactionary preaching that has been the downfall of many good men. He must seek never to preach *about* people, as is so customary, but to preach truth. So often men see something or hear something that sets them off, or as the young people say, "turns them on."

This is a time for courage and timid souls will perish in today's world. The seeking layman is hungry for a courageous pastor because many pastors have been so cowed for so many years. Many good and well-meaning church members are not active because their leaders are not courageous men. A few men have already lost their jobs because of pulpit utterances or for standing up to power blocs within their churches; many more will lose their jobs before the pulpit is redeemed in some sections. Many men braved the threat of racial prejudice and asked for open-door policies in Southern churches. Some lost their jobs, but some rallied a better and more rational element within the church membership. Many laymen are ready and eager to have a pastor question the power structures within the congregation and to free the churches from the control of the few. There would be more support than most pastors dare think if they would step out on faith and really preach their convictions. The one group that talks the most about faith, more than likely has the least when it comes to courage. Many are courageous but too many lack this one great quality.

No discussion of genuineness would be complete without some word concerning the fact that we as pastors cannot blame laymen for putting us into a bowl. If in this book we have sounded as if the plight of the pastoral ministry is the fault of the laymen this has been grossly misleading. The first people to set up false images and behavioral patterns are that group called pastors. We have played roles handed down to us by older men in the ministry and we have not been courageous to change them. Certainly it is true that these images and expected patterns are in the laymen's minds but our own group put them there. We have painted ourselves into a corner and we have had to live in a goldfish bowl world because we desired to jump in!

Back yonder in the distant past somewhere when all this confusion started as to the duties and work of the pastoral ministry, someone or perhaps an entire generation of men refused to be honest and to tell the people what was in their hearts. However, it is too late now to lament over the past and since the patterns of expectation are here the thing we must do now is to explain to our people quite frankly and honestly the things about our roles that bind us and that have unnecessary strangle holds on us. When we do this we shall have to expect hostility because some are going to remind us that dear old brother Smith visited and "sat-a-spell" with all the folks. It is going to take real diplomacy, real courage and above all, firmness to break the mold; we must do it or the church is going to be in dire need of men for this calling of the pastorate.

One such pastor was so overworked with his demands that he told his congregation quite frankly that he could not stand the midweek service and that it was a thing of the past. His people surprised him and voted unanimously to drop it from the schedule. His honesty provoked them to compassion and understanding.

If we resent so much pressure from the denomination and from the demands to get converts, it is our obligation to talk this over quite frankly with our people and it will surprise many pastors to discover how sympathetic their people can be. We can only get out of the bowl if we want out because we jumped in, and even though that might have been an unconscious act on our part, we can consciously get out of it now if we have the fortitude.

In the next place we have been intellectually dishonest with our people and time has caught up with us. Just because we say things from the pulpit doesn't automatically mean that the laymen believe them to be true. We are going to have to study long and arduously and stay abreast of such things as the scientific inquiry into evolution and the Genesis narratives. This is only *one* example and there are many others, but the point is that our people need to be led intellectually from the pulpit as they are led intellectually from every other quarter of modern life. People are hungry for pastors who are not only abreast but able to interpret the maze of theological unrest such as is created by the "God is dead" movement and other controversies. Laymen are interested in an intellectual approach to religion as never before and the pastoral ministry must be courageous enough to lead.

In the final analysis he who would be genuine shall have many followers. Many of our young men will give themselves for service in the pastoral ministry if they can see pioneering attitudes put into a proper focus. If our people see that we are sincere in providing better images and avenues of pastoral service, it will not be long before they too will change with us because dynamic and courageous love gives birth to the same qualities. If our churches are corrupt and if the life of many pastors is a vicious struggle for survival then we must be about the business of changing it. There is not a congregation anywhere that does not have a sufficient number of people to do all the things we have mentioned because they are probably sicker of the goldfish bowl than we who are in it.

We can have a rebirth of this work if a few men will

come forward and lead, but as was pointed out earlier in this chapter, we must correctly assess the situation and the church must cease being used by pastor and people for personal ego needs. Some pastors have played one congregation against another for higher salaries or bigger positions. On the other hand, the layman must stop wanting a show and demanding that his pastor be a showman. He must want a priest, an overseer of his soul, a brother, a friend, a guiding spirit and intellect for his spiritual needs and those of his dear family.

No one is asking to get out of the water or out of the other work of the pastorate when he seeks to be free or when he begs for understanding. Those who want out of bowl *and* water are rapidly leaving but many older men are desirous that their remaining years be productive and that they not be shelved in favor of a better "showman" in the years when they can offer the most in mature wisdom.

If we despise the cult tag, let us arise and change it and free ourselves from its corrosive influence. Let us renew the pastoral office as it directly relates to laymen. Someone has got to tell the truth about the man in the goldfish bowl, his dilemma and his wish for fulfillment, but first the burden is on him, the burden of honesty and genuineness. Perhaps when God's people see themselves as the pastor sees them and when pastors see themselves as the people see them the blind will not lead the blind but, because of newer insights, both will join hands for a rebuilding of the importance of both pulpit and pew.